Things Lost In The
FIRE

What A Fire Doesn't Consume It Purifies

LaDonyae Thomas

Things Lost In The Fire:
What A Fire Doesn't Consume It Purifies

Copyright © 2023 LaDonyae Thomas

This book is a work of non-fiction. Some names and identifying details have not been mentioned or changed to protect the privacy of individuals. Other names are used as they appear in the author's memory. The images included in this work are either the property of the author or used with permission, and some have been altered or blurred to maintain the privacy of the individuals depicted.

ISBN: 979-8-218-34067-4 Paperback
Published by: The Pen of A Ready Writer Publishing
Email: areadywriterpublishing@gmail.com
Printed in U.S.A.

Things Lost In The

FIRE

What A Fire Doesn't Consume It Purifies

LaDonyae Thomas

The Pen Of A Ready Writer Publishing
P.O. Box 5886, Lake Charles, LA 70606

Dedicated To

Those who have endured trials in silence, their stories untold but their strength undeniable. May these pages inspire the courage to share your own journey of survival.

Table of Contents

LOSS

GRIEF

family gatherings

In Loving Memory of

Donald Ray
THOMAS, JR.
'DJ'

MISSOURI
'MISSY'
Thomas

IDEAS

Divorce

- release

- new mindset

- false beliefs

FAITH

friendships

LOSS
LOSS
LOSS

NEW BEGINNINGS

RESTORATION

FAITH

BUSINESS  HOPE

Beauty For Ashes....

To appoint unto them that mourn in Zion, to give unto them beauty for ashes, the oil of joy for mourning, the garment of praise for the spirit of heaviness; that they might be called trees of righteousness, the planting of the Lord, that he might be glorified. -Isaiah 61:3

God is a Consuming Fire...

27. The words "once more" indicate the removing of what can be shaken—that is, created things—so that what cannot be shaken may remain.

28. Therefore, since we are receiving a kingdom that cannot be shaken, let us be thankful, and so worship God acceptably with reverence and awe,

29. for our "God is a consuming fire

-Hebrews 12:27-29, AMP

Breaking Silence:

Healing Wounds

I open my scars to let them breathe,
They have been hidden, needing some care.
Looking deep inside, seeing what is beneath,
The scars, the wounds, it is all there

There is hurt hidden, not easy to see,
Tucked away in corners, never spoken.
Now I'm cleaning it out, setting it free,
Memories flood back, but I'm not broken.

This time, the scars stay open to heal,
I'm ready for the pain, ready for the end.
New chapters, new doors, they feel real,
I can speak now, I won't bend.

Gone are the days of silent, empty phrases,
I will soar in life's vast, open spaces.
Welcoming the morning's warm embraces,
As I leave behind the night, with all its traces.

The end of pain, the start of new,
I'm ready, I'm strong, I'll get through.

LaDonyae Thomas

Preface

The journey of life takes unexpected turns, bringing us to crossroads that forever changed our path. This memoir captures some of those pivotal moments that tested my faith and reshaped my spirit over an eight-year period. It is not a chronological story from beginning to end but rather glimpses into the challenging yet transformative experiences that were the flames that refined and strengthened me.

Through the fire of adversity, a new self emerged. What follows are the pivotal moments, the times of personal trial and loss over this eight-year journey, that forever marked my faith's path. From profound struggles within my marriage to the devastating deaths of loved ones, these experiences ignited fires of change. The heat purified my spirit, shedding old versions of myself and bringing deeper truth to light.

Join me as I reflect on these touching episodes that refined my life's purpose and built an unshakeable faith from within. The ashes from the fire reveal who I am meant to become, and what remains is what was meant to stay.

Prelude

Two years have passed since I started putting these words on paper, seeking healing in their release. But some pains are too deep for quick relief. Though time takes the sharpest sting away, the ache inside endures.

While writing this memoir, I was not just bleeding onto a blank page; I was bleeding in a place of healing, where I wasn't just stepping in my own pool and leaving tracks. I am now bleeding at the doctor's office. This doctor is my faith in God, He guides me as I write, giving me strength with every word. I have now made a decision: I have decided to open my wounds and no longer keep them only to myself. This is the place where I can freely bleed and there's help. He guides me as I write, giving me strength with every pen stroke, every tap of a key. The healing has begun.

Since I am a private person, sharing openly does not come naturally to me - it requires welcoming others into the vulnerable parts of my story that I have always kept closely guarded. For so long, I kept my pain hidden, never sharing my story. My pain was a private cycle - unseen wounds leaving tracks only I could follow.

But now, opening these wounds and bleeding them onto the page allows me to finally heal and move forward. As I pour out my truth, it is God who soothes my wounds, attending to the hurt. What good is a wound if it's kept hidden and unattended?

This memoir details my journey through the fire of loss – the loss of my voice, relationships, material things, motherly role, and so much more. Like a raging fire, it consumed the contents of my life, leaving only ashes behind. Yet even a destructive blaze has a purifying purpose. My story is meant to be shared, so that I, and others, may find healing. There is comfort in sharing openly, revealing my truth without shame. The sharing of pain releases its grip. As I open myself to compassion, God empathetically attends to my wounds.

From the ashes, I will rise stronger, purified but not destroyed. The fire burns away only what must be relinquished. A new life awaits on the other side. As the scripture says, "He gives us beauty for ashes." From the ruins, beauty will bloom again.

For I, saith the LORD,
will be unto her a wall of fire round about,
and will be the glory in the midst of her.
- Zechariah 2:5

Things Lost In The Fire

Chapter 1

Ignite and Transform

For I, saith the LORD, will be unto her a wall of fire round about and will be the glory in the midst of her. - Zechariah 2:5

L ittle did I know, as these years of transformation unfolded, they would lead me down a path of self-examination and spiritual awakening.

The year was 2014 and I found myself wrestling with a strong attraction that I didn't expect. This was just the beginning of a series of life-changing experiences that would challenge my faith and strength in ways I didn't realize. These challenges tested me, burning away the old me and revealing a new, stronger self.

This unexpected attraction was toward another man. This person was handsome, a leader, and a nice dresser. The issue was that I was already married and so was he. I couldn't understand how someone so filled with the Holy Spirit and the power of God, so anointed, could have thoughts and desires for someone other than their spouse. I felt an internal battle, a conflict that shook the very core of my faith.

What was wrong with me? What was going on inside that a woman of God like me could even think about adultery? But the reality was, I was feeling this way, even though no one else knew. It was a secret struggle, hidden within the chambers of my heart.

I couldn't comprehend it. It became a battle within myself, trying to find a reason and understand why I, someone who studied the Word of God so deeply, could have such impure thoughts. The scriptures told me, that although I had not acted on these thoughts, just having those thoughts is a sin. I felt unworthy. I would sit in the church pulpit, reminding myself of how impure I was for having these thoughts and how I felt I didn't deserve to be sitting in such a sacred place. It was my hidden reality, but I couldn't hide it from myself. While I battled with this conflict, I became fully aware that the man's feelings for me were mutual.

I didn't know what to do. I couldn't share this with my friend; she would see me differently. I didn't feel comfortable speaking with my pastor; they might condemn me and ask me to step down from ministry. Talking to my husband wasn't an option either; it would hurt his ego. The only thing I knew to do was to pray. I remembered my pastor's voice at that time about crying out in prayer, laying everything before God. My pastor would teach us specific instructions on how he thought we should always pray. I tried this, but it felt like a ritual rather than a sincere act. I was doing what I had been taught, and it was supposed to work, right? But it didn't feel natural, and the thoughts and emotions wouldn't go away.

Two forces were battling inside me. My faith, which made me feel ashamed, and my sincere feelings for another man. This struggle was more than personal, it was about the conflict between what I was taught to believe and what I truly felt.

I continued to pray, study the word, and attend church services. But the ache inside me persisted. I couldn't believe that a woman of my stature was struggling with such thoughts.

I needed to shift my prayers, so I decided to dedicate some time at the church's altar for five days during my lunch break at work. I was alone at the altar. It was a struggle for the first two days, but I continued consistently until I received my breakthrough.

In my journey of self-reflection, I realized it wasn't just about praying; it was about truly understanding the underlying issues within me. Prayer is a vital tool for communicating with God, but at that moment, I found myself talking more than listening. To get to the root of my feelings, I had to look deep inside. I've always been attracted to men who are strong leaders, who represent authority. This attraction wasn't just to the man himself, but to his spirit of leadership.

I had been married for eleven years and I felt a lack of this type of leadership within my husband. Although he was a supervisor at his job he didn't carry that role into our home. This left me frequently stepping in to correct and manage things, a role I didn't feel was meant for me. This gap in our marriage led me to be attracted to another man who I believed demonstrated authority. He was a supervisor who led effortlessly, an obvious contrast to my husband, who struggled with decision-making and clear communication.

I've always shown leadership qualities myself, from being a minister to having a history of holding various supervisory roles. However, I never desired to be the leader of my family.

This attraction to another man highlighted a missing piece in my marriage, a realization that was difficult to accept. Although I understood this, I knew it wasn't right. I could not change my husband's leadership style, but I could hold myself accountable for my thoughts.

Looking back, I now realize that this internal turmoil served as a pivotal moment in my journey. Eventually, these internal flames of attraction dimmed as I continued to pursue my passion and faith in Christ. At the time, I had no idea that God was using these inner struggles to ignite a transformative fire within me. He was preparing me for a deeper level of anointing and a profound journey, and to do so, He needed me to be aware of the things I didn't even know existed within me. God was on to something, and He needed those parts of me to die so that I could truly live and embrace a more profound level of anointing for the journey He had in store.

During this time, I resided in Jasper, Texas and I made a bold decision to stop wearing only skirts and dresses but rather wear pants again after a decade. This decision was made just a few months after my self-discovery. I was nervous about how people would react, especially my church family. I wondered if they might view it as losing my faith, slipping back into a worldly life. But the truth was, those church dresses restricted me.

While dealing with my inner conflicts and rethinking my beliefs and desires, I realized that I was also questioning the strict rules in my life. This led me to wonder why I decided to follow only wearing skirts and dresses.

At the time I worked as a Parent Educator and dresses didn't fit the active nature of engaging with children, such as sitting on the floor, running around, and playing on the playground. The dresses limited my ability to fully participate.

Looking back on my challenging journey, I understood that the changes in me were not only about my feelings and spirituality but also about practical aspects of my life. This made me rethink important things in my faith, including why I believed I should only wear skirts and dresses.

I thought, 'Would people assume I was falling into sin?' That's what my pastors preached - any step backward meant sliding toward sin. But was it truly sinful, I wondered, or merely a man-made religious rule?

During this period of profound personal change, where I was shedding old beliefs and embracing a truer version of myself, my decision to start wearing pants again became symbolic. It was an outward manifestation of my inner transformation – a liberation from unnecessary restrictions, not just in how I thought and felt, but also in how I presented myself.

My experience was about freeing myself, not just from the secret struggles I faced but also from all the unexamined rules that had controlled my life. Embracing pants was not just a change in fashion; it represented a step towards aligning my external presentation with my internal growth.

My pastors often quoted Deuteronomy 22:5, claiming it prohibited women from wearing pants. They suggested a woman wearing pants, which were deemed as men's clothing was an abomination. However, I came to understand the verse differently. It meant condemnation of cross-dressing, men wearing women's clothes, and vice versa.

So, I began wearing pants to work. It shocked some coworkers, and puzzled others, fueling gossip and accusations. Thankfully, my husband was understanding and helped me feel better about my decision. Wearing pants gave me a sense of freedom, yet I remained concerned about what others thought, especially my pastors. I felt like I was breaking from a belief system that had trapped so many. How could God condemn me to hell for wearing women's pants? If this verse bans women from wearing pants, what does it mean for cultures that wear robes that resemble dresses that are worn by both genders? These were the questions I asked myself as I searched for the answers.

What I discovered was that removing myself from only wearing skirts was about more than just clothes. It was about removing restrictions that limited me and man-made ideologies that contained me. I still believe there are distinctions between men and women clothing and that women should dress femininely. However, this change was more about God removing parts of me that were hindrances.

Women's pants are specifically tailored to fit a woman's body, just as a woman's bra and underwear are designed for a woman's anatomy. Men have their versions tailored to their shape as well. So, all pants are not exclusively for one gender, just like all undergarments are not exclusive to one gender.

When we closely examine the scripture, it prohibits cross-dressing for both men and women, not only women. Yet somehow the interpretation is often solely focused on women wearing pants, missing the instruction for men.

If this scripture truly means women can never wear pants because they are only for men, then it would also mean men can never wear robes, kilts, or anything that resembles dresses. God designed women to solely have breasts, so a man wearing a woman's bra, for example, would be considered an abomination because it is not a body part naturally designed for a man.

Now that I had a better understanding of the scripture I felt like I had removed a layer of traditional beliefs that had been restricting my walk with God. It baffled me that such a belief could exist that would suggest wearing pants, regardless of the depth of my relationship with God, could render my entire relationship with Him irrelevant.

Looking back at specific moments in 2014, it was a year that challenged and shaped me into a stronger version of myself. It felt like a fire burning inside, consuming parts of me I was accustomed to cherishing. During that time, I grappled with confusing feelings, as if I was losing a part of who I thought I was.

The attraction I struggled with was like losing my innocence, veering off the path I thought I should follow. Those inner desires, though intangible, changed the idealized image I had of myself.

In a way, this struggle was like a fire, burning away my old ideas and making me face the complexities of being human. It was a turning point, testing my faith and revealing a new me.

I recognize that many Godly women choose to solely wear dresses and skirts, including some incredibly powerful and anointed women I respect. My stance comes from my convictions, for which I know there are firm biblical grounds. Still, for me, this awakening regarding the scripture's true meaning and intent has been profoundly liberating.

In the journey of faith, the terrain often shifts beneath our feet, prompting us to reassess beliefs we once held as absolute truth. As gold emerges refined from flames, I arose from that pivotal year remade, with deeper convictions rooted not in others' teachings, but in my own lived understanding of God and what it means to walk truly in His ways.

Chapter 2

Fiery Trials of Faith

These have come so that the proven genuineness of your faith—of greater worth than gold, which perishes even though refined by fire—may result in praise, glory, and honor, when Jesus Christ is revealed. -I Peter 1:7

In 2016, my husband lost his job where he was employed by the Texas Department Of Criminal Justice for eighteen years. Shortly afterward, our mortgage company was acquired by another loan servicer which led to an unexpected increase in our monthly payments. This increase was due to the new company adding escrow, despite our fixed mortgage agreement and the fact that escrow inclusion isn't mandatory in Texas. I contested this with the servicer, but my efforts were to no avail.

The loss of our primary income, coupled with the increased mortgage payments, placed us in a difficult financial situation. We applied for a loan modification twice, but both requests were denied. When we attempted to continue our regular payments according to our mortgage contract, the company refused to apply the full payments toward our monthly mortgage. They continued to insist on including the escrow. Although my husband had a part-time job we were still struggling financially, the job he lost was our main source of income. We could barely afford the original mortgage amount, let alone the additional escrow.

The situation worsened when the company began holding our payments without applying them to the mortgage. Despite knowing their actions contradicted our contract and were likely illegal, we couldn't afford legal representation. To make matters worse, later on, we missed two mortgage payments. In September 2017, I called to try to make a partial payment, but it was refused. By this point, we were not only behind on two payments but also burdened with several months of unapplied escrow. This led to us receiving a notification for foreclosure in January 2018.

The foreclosure was a devastating blow. My husband, having already lost his job, now felt he had lost his dignity. Despite the result of the foreclosure, I never blamed him, although I could not help but recall the events of 2016 that led to his job loss. He was a lieutenant then, aspiring to become a captain. We attended revival services where it was prophesied he would become a captain. He was already working closer to home, but he wasn't satisfied because his heart was set on the captain position, which would have given him weekends off. I remember telling him that God had revealed to me his season for the position was no longer available for him, but he struggled to accept this.

Ignoring the prophecy and without discussing it with me, he transferred back to his former unit in another city, hoping for a promotion. I only learned about this decision on his last day when he returned from a farewell celebration at work. I felt disrespected and upset; he had made a significant decision without involving me, a decision that everyone else knew about except for me, his wife. His return to the former unit was associated with many problems, and just eight months later, in October 2016, he was fired.

At this critical moment, I was employed by Texas Health and Human Services, undergoing training from Monday through Friday. While training, my job covered my weekly hotel stays.

During this transformative period, I sought advice from my pastor's wife about our next steps. Housing options in Jasper were limited, and she mentioned an old, abandoned house owned by my friend's husband. My friend warned me about the house's condition, noting its long vacancy and lack of air conditioning and she did not feel it was a suitable option for our family. I then contemplated having my family join me at the hotel, funded by my job, as a temporary solution. However, this posed challenges, as my children were attending school in Jasper, and the hotel in Beaumont was an hour drive away.

This plan was abruptly derailed just two days later when I was unexpectedly fired from my job. I remember that day vividly; we had just finished a few days of training that week and I returned to my office in Jasper. My spirit immediately discerned the atmosphere at my job wasn't right. While sitting in my office, I texted my husband, sharing with him that I felt I would be fired that day. Gazing out the window, the vision of my dismissal played in my mind. Later that day, I met my new supervisor for the first time. She summoned me to her office, and before she could complete her sentence, I interrupted, "I already know, I'm getting terminated today." Her shocked expression revealed her surprise. When she asked how I knew, I avoided mentioning the word "vision" and simply said I had dreamt it.

The plan for my family to stay with me at the hotel was no longer an option.

These unexpected turn of events, starting with the loss of my husband's job, set off a chain of challenges for us, the first of which was facing the harsh reality of our living situation. The loss of his job was like a spark that set the blaze guiding us towards a new beginning as we began to prepare ourselves to search for a new home.

In 2005, I had a dream that vividly showed me this house, paving the way for me to become a homeowner at just 24 years old. Built the following year, with its four bedrooms and two bathrooms, it was the exact embodiment of that dream, down to its exterior color. On the property, we planted lemon and plum trees, which grew alongside our family. This house wasn't just our first owned home; it was a sanctuary of sorts, where many nights were spent pacing the floors in deep prayer. Those walls absorbed countless prayers, echoing the hopes, dreams, and challenges we faced during our time there. As we prepared to leave, it was clear we were not just leaving a building, but a significant chapter of our life, filled with memories and milestones.

On our final day there, a home where we had lived for twelve years, a blend of sadness and unexpected excitement filled me. Leaving this house, rich with memories, was not easy. Every corner reminded me of the life we had built there. Despite how I felt, there was a sense of anticipation for the new chapter ahead.

I had the choice to be angry with my husband over his job loss and to question his faith decisions. It would have been easy to let out my frustrations, but it would only add more trouble to our lives. I knew that wouldn't solve anything. Arguing would have only increased the pain, especially for our children, who were already dealing with so much change. It would have been like adding fuel to the fire.

I understood my temperament, so in that moment, I chose what was best for my mental state—I chose silence. Our family needed unity and no additional conflict. My anger would have shaken the stability I was trying to maintain for our kids. Although my anger may have been justified, I understood that if I was led by anger, I would not have been led by God. A wise decision is never made in anger. James 1:20 reminds us that anger does not produce the righteousness of God, so my response would have made the situation worse.

As we prepared for the move, gathering boxes and collecting our things, a deep sadness filled the atmosphere, especially among our children.

On that last day, in my empty bedroom closet, I found a moment of peace in prayer. While sitting in the closet, I recorded a song, a symbol of hope and new beginnings. It was a reminder that even with endings, there's always a chance to start new.

In the stillness of that empty room, my heart found its rhythm in the melody of that song, a gentle yet profound reminder that every ending paves the way for a new beginning. As I closed the chapter of our life in that house and stepped into the unknown, guided by faith and uncertain of our next destination, I knew we were not just leaving a place, but moving forward under God's guidance. It was an exit from that story of my life.

Chapter 3

Refining Fire of Faith

But He knoweth the way that I take: when He hath tried me,
I shall come forth as gold. -Job 23:10 KJV

In February 2018, as a result of the foreclosure notice compelled us to search for a new home. We were uncertain about our situation, so we prayed for guidance. We weighed our options, considering various locations in Jasper and the possibility of moving to Tyler or Lufkin, Texas. Despite not knowing the exact direction of where we needed to go, we decided to begin our search and we eventually decided to explore housing opportunities in Lufkin.

While driving around Lufkin, I asked God if it was His will for me to be in Lukin to provide me with a job there. Within just a short time God responded. During the house search, I received a phone call from a recruiter. The day I received that phone call I knew it was divine intervention.

It was a pleasant day with mild outdoor temperatures. My husband and I had been praying and having discussions all day as we drove during our house search.

As the recruiter began to speak I felt a sense of anticipation. Months prior, I had applied for the role of Outreach Marketing Specialist, a position I had forgotten about. She stated she was impressed with my resume but noticed the location said Jasper, the position was searching for a candidate who lived in or near Nacogdoches. I explained that we were currently house hunting in Lufkin, and Nacogdoches was approximately twenty minutes away. The recruiter's voice filled with enthusiasm as if she had taken a deep breath of fresh air. The recruiter decided to forward my application to the hiring manager. This was the answer to my prayer. God's plan was being fulfilled.

After getting the phone call from the recruiter expressing interest in my qualifications, our house search took on an even greater sense of anticipation and excitement. Even though I did not have a formal job offer yet, just receiving that initial call filled me with renewed optimism.

Later, we found a house in Lufkin. It was slightly outside the city limits, in a peaceful, quiet neighborhood, with plenty of backyard space, and a garage. Despite being fifteen other applicants, the real estate company chose us. Again, another divine move of God. Once again God had given us favor over all the other applicants, our names were pushed to the top of the list. I was reminded of Psalm 5:12 which states, that God surrounds the righteous with His divine favor like a protective shield. Feeling deeply grateful, I saw this moment as a clear manifestation of that promise, a tangible experience of His protective favor in our lives.

Excited by this blessing, I immediately called my pastor's wife to share the news. However, her response of simply asking 'How much is the rent?' dampened my excitement. Wanting to maintain my joyful spirit, I quickly ended the call to focus instead on the positive aspects of the new chapter of our lives.

We knew this move was a move of God because everything began to happen speedily. Everything seemed to fall into place, except our church was approximately sixty miles away from our new home. We faithfully drove from Lufkin to Jasper every Sunday for church services for nine months.

Our three children stayed with my parents in Jasper for three weeks until Spring break, finishing their school term before joining us in Lufkin.

In March, the company I had interacted with during our house search contacted me for an interview. This brought to mind my first encounter with this company while I lived in Jasper back in 2016, when I first applied for and interviewed for a different position. At that time, I had a dream about working there and its benefits package, but I didn't get the job. I realized it was a matter of wrong timing and location. Two years later, in 2018, after moving to a new city, the opportunity with the same company resurfaced, aligning with God's timing and not mine.

After a successful interview in 2018, I was hired and started working in April. The hiring manager told me the position had been vacant for five months and he was excited, saying he had 'finally found the right person with the skills for the job.' I took this as a sign that the job was meant for me, but it required me to move first before I could receive it.

Despite the job's good pay and corporate setting, God had revealed to me that my time there would only last for two years. I then shared this divine insight with my friend. I am accustomed to God giving me "secret intel" that frequently communicates with me through numbers like two and three. Therefore, I understood this two-year employment as His divine plan.

The job was rewarding in many ways. I worked from home, traveled to assigned counties, had access to two personal company credit cards, and occasionally stayed in hotels for travel. It also offered unique opportunities, such as renting cars for work trips and organizing community events. Through this role, I was introduced to various local and state government officials, which was an entire new experience for me.

Looking back, I see how God was strategic throughout this period. Those two years were not just about the job itself; they were a time of preparation for the future. God wanted me to gain experience in interacting with community officials, a skill that would be important later. At the time, I didn't fully grasp that this job was God's way of training me for the plans He had in store. Throughout my time there, I received significant favors from my supervisor, evidenced by two pay raises, affirming that I was in the right season.

As my professional life was flourishing, my personal life faced challenges. The success and attention I received at work caused jealousy in my husband. It was common for him to be jealous, however, his jealousy concerning my new position intensified. He was particularly uncomfortable with my interactions with men, leading to disagreements. In one incident, when a work call had extended five minutes past 5 PM, he insisted I end it immediately.

My husband's jealousy concerns were escalating. When my colleagues and I gathered for retreats or trainings, he insisted I not ride with any male coworkers, even if female coworkers were also present. During these events, he demanded I call him on every lunch break. There were times when I didn't call due to engaging in conversations with coworkers. However, this was unacceptable to him, causing disagreements.

My husband's growing jealousy, like a shadow, began to darken the light of my professional achievements. The more I flourished at work, the more his insecurity manifested in suffocating surveillance. There were evenings when the joy of a successful day was extinguished with a barrage of suspicion when I attempted to tell him about my day which included the news about meeting the mayor in one of my assigned counties.

Then one night I had a dream. In it, I was extremely happy with a husband, though God didn't reveal his face. In the dream was an unexplainable joy and meek, humble spirit within me. This husband in the dream was loving, and I was utterly submissive toward him.

I was confused as to why God would give me a dream about another husband when I was already married. This dream wasn't lustful, nor did it show me committing infidelity; it depicted me with another man whom I was married to. Yet, I knew the revelatory nature of my dreams. I wanted to share it with my friend and get an interpretation from my pastor's wife, but I knew their perception of me would change entirely. Although my friend knew the divine nature of my dreams, I felt with this particular dream she wouldn't understand. It wasn't that I desired another man, but the dream left me wondering what secret intel God was trying to reveal to me. We could never fathom nor articulate the mind of God; it was something I couldn't explain. However, it was something I kept in remembrance.

After two days, I finally revealed the dream to my husband one night in our bedroom. I explained how in the dream, I was happy in a marriage. He didn't respond at all, highly unusual for him. But I knew in my spirit that the faceless man in the dream was not him.

By this time, I had been employed at my new job for one year. My husband's possessiveness had sprouted wildly, choking our relationship. I remember once, at a community event he attended with me I was casually discussing insurance with a salesman. My husband watched from afar, his body tense with unfounded jealousy. That evening at home our argument was fierce, as I confronted him about his unreasonable behavior.

Our home, which had always been a solid foundation of prayer now felt fractured. He accused me of flirting at the event, but no matter how much I tried to explain the innocence of the interaction, he refused to see reason. His surveillance of me had become unbearable. He began sifting through my belongings while I was away on trips expecting to find evidence of wrongdoing. The thought that he still doubted my loyalty after all those years twisted painfully inside me.

One day he entered the door returning home from work and his mere presence triggered a wave of disgust in me. It was at that moment I recognized the spirit of bitterness attempting to take hold. I was reminded of the scripture, Hebrews 12:15, I understood the warning against letting a 'root of bitterness' grow, aware of the trouble it could cause and how it could defile me. I knew that if I did not tame this emotion, it had the potential to grow into a destructive force. Despite my efforts and prayers for our marriage, I couldn't bridge the mistrust he had created.

His jealousy began to mentally exhaust me. I no longer looked forward to coming home. I began purposely scheduling events that allowed me to travel so I could stay overnight in a hotel to have peace.

At this point, I started feeling that our marriage was heading in the wrong direction. Moving to Lufkin was meant to be a positive, God-led change, but things were getting worse. I started reflecting on all the experiences I had quietly endured over the years, the issues I felt I couldn't discuss. There were so many matters I believed I couldn't share with my church community, as I was supposed to bear them and fulfill my duties as a wife. Inside me, there was a multitude of feelings and thoughts I needed to express, but obligations and expectations led me to suppress my voice for a long time.

The accumulating weight of these unspoken challenges began to shift my perspective. I found myself not wanting to be married anymore. My husband's constant accusations of cheating and his odd behavior were too much. Despite him being the father of my children, essentially a good man, the magnitude of our issues were growing. I had always believed in our growth together, envisioning a marriage where both partners understood that growth is essential to maintaining balance in a relationship; it's about adapting to each other's needs and perspectives. But in our case, it felt like we were moving in opposite directions, with each step widening the gap between us, as we struggled to align our individual paths and expectations.

By September 2019, I made the difficult decision to file for divorce. It wasn't just his jealousy that led me here; it was a culmination of many challenges I had silently endured over the years. Before reaching this conclusion, I spent a lot of time thinking it over. The final push came when I discovered in his phone that he had been communicating with two women. I took screenshots as evidence, which ultimately confirmed my decision to file.

Around this time, we are now approaching 2020 drawing closer to my second work anniversary.

In 2020, the situation at work changed. My department shifted from the community sector to Medicare, leading to significant challenges. Company agents began working in my assigned counties, creating tension with organizations that preferred partnering with me. These agents and their supervisors, frustrated by the organization's preference, started spreading fabrications about me in an attempt to tarnish my reputation. My once supportive supervisor began considering disciplinary actions against me based on their baseless claims.

My actions were now under close scrutiny. On one occasion, I had scheduled a community event with a particular organization. When I arrived, no one was there, which was against policy. Feeling pressed in my spirit and anticipating accusations, I took pictures of the building and parking lot as proof of my presence. I also called a colleague as a witness.

When I returned to my desk, I made notes in the system that I showed up and no one was there. A week later, my supervisor contacted me because the supervisor of an agent went to check behind me concerning my events. Regarding that particular event, she claimed to have contacted the organization and it was stated they never spoke with me nor scheduled an event.

I communicated to my supervisor that I had documented all event details in Salesforce, including the contact information, and I had photographic evidence of my arrival at the venue where no one was present. Additionally, I kept the receipt for the gas purchase made with the company's credit card. Despite all the evidence, there were false allegations claiming that the organization had no communication with me regarding the event. My supervisor, despite having access to all my documentation, felt compelled to formally address these claims due to pressure from his superior.

The agents and their supervisor continued to target me weekly and would not stop. It was as if finding allegations against me became their new job role. I understood my season there was ending as I neared God's revealed two-year timeframe. I had now passed that mark, staying a few months longer than God's appointed time. It became noticeably clear I had overstayed the time that God allotted. My trials intensified the longer I remained. It was almost like food left cooking for too long under the heat - the overextension started to affect me. The constantly fabricated allegations had become exhausting. Still, I persisted in responding to every false allegation with proof, even as it was clear my time there was ending.

Things continued to get intense. On another occasion, my supervisor couldn't leave a voicemail because my personal cellphone's mailbox was full, leading to a write-up for being unreachable, a move I knew was to satisfy his superiors. Recognizing I was under attack, I continued to meticulously document everything. Despite the continuous fabrications by the agents, the investigations always proved their allegations to be false. The situation escalated to the point where I had to report it to HR, who also deemed the accusations against me as absurd.

Things began to get really intense as I passed the two-year mark at my job. I began to receive ridiculous write-ups from my supervisor, who was trying to please his boss by appearing to handle me as his subordinate.

Feeling overwhelmed, I took some time off work as per my doctor's orders. During this break, I decided to figure out my next steps. I prayed and sought guidance from God, who instructed me to become a notary, take a loan signing course, and become a tax preparer to start my own business. With years of experience in tax preparation, this seemed like a great plan. I took the necessary courses, registered my business as an LLC with the state, and then returned to work.

I vividly remember the moment that led to my resignation in December 2020. While praying and pacing in my living room, I reached the end of my rug. It was in this spot, turning at the rug's edge, that I received profound communication from God. He spoke promising me I would have multiple streams of income. This spiritual encounter reassured me about my future, guiding me towards leaving my job and following the path as an entrepreneur, in line with the divine promise I felt was given to me.

As I decided to resign, I wasn't certain when or how God would fulfill His promise. It wasn't my responsibility to figure out the details; it was God's, and my role was to trust Him and His Word. Isaiah 55:11 states, "So is my word that goes out from my mouth: it will not return to me empty but will accomplish what I desire and achieve the purpose for which I sent it." This scripture reminds us that God's Word is powerful and always fulfills its purpose.

As the trials at work intensified in late 2020 after passing my two-year mark there, the challenges and trials seemed unending. False accusations, relentless scrutiny, and a growing sense of unease had become the norm. God was refining me through the fire of adversity for a purpose. Though the way forward remained unclear at the moment, I understood difficult seasons of pruning often prepare our character for blossoming. I resolved to walk in hopeful expectancy toward the doors I knew God soon would open, believing the promising words He spoke over my life, one that would lead me to trust in God's promise of multiple streams of income. Where He guides me, He provides.

In this journey, the importance of obedience to God's guidance is emphasized. By listening to His voice and seeking His direction, one navigates life's paths with greater assurance and fewer hardships. Although obedience doesn't shield us from life's challenges or attacks, it does guarantee God's protection and presence. This underlines the importance of adhering to divine guidance, especially during tough times, as it guides us on a protected and meaningful path where every challenge we face is an integral part of a greater, divinely orchestrated plan.

When faith faces the furnace of adversity, it becomes a resilient shield against life's fiery trials.

Chapter 4

Beauty For Ashes

To appoint unto them that mourn in Zion, to give unto them beauty for ashes, the oil of joy for mourning, the garment of praise for the spirit of heaviness; that they might be called trees of righteousness, the planting of the Lord, that he might be glorified -Isaiah 61:3, KJV

This chapter of my life details the bonds of marriage, faith, and self-discovery that were tested in ways I could never have imagined. As I rewind the tapestry of my memories to the early years of my marriage, It took me through a journey of unexpected revelations, complex emotions, and the quiet struggles that often go unseen.

To many, my husband and I were seen as the ideal couple. We attended church services regularly and were always seen together as a family. Others often desired to have a marriage like ours as we appeared to be the epitome of marriages. However, just like most couples, we had our differences. Prayer had once been our strong foundation was now unbalanced. It's important in the oneness of marriage that something as profound as prayer is maintained as a routine for both partners. I understood it took both of us to pray and remain dependent on one another when a marriage consists of two.

We were married in January 2003. Our journey began under complex circumstances; we welcomed our first child together in February 2001, before marriage. In January 2004, almost a year after our wedding, our family expanded quickly with the birth of our second child. During these personal milestones, I was operating a business from home, creating floral arrangements and home décor. I also enrolled in college for the first time in 2003, embracing both academic and familial responsibilities.

Our marriage faced unexpected challenges early on. In 2004, shortly after the birth of our second child, I discovered the existence of my husband's five-year-old daughter, a child he had never mentioned before. This news came as a surprise, altering the dynamics of our growing family. His oldest son, who was now seven, was six years old when we married, he had already been a part of our family.

My husband was a complex man, good in many ways and the father of our three children, however, he placed heavy demands on me. He relied on me to remember everything for him, often telling people I was his 'brain.' A word he often jokingly said, but a term I disliked. He often bragged to others about my role as a wife and I always made sure he left for work with everything he needed, including meals I had prepared. Despite these efforts, the appreciation I needed was missing.

I had endured years of my husband's jealousy. He was so insecure that I couldn't even sit alone on a hill in our backyard without his interference. His intrusions extended to my most private moments, like when I retreated to my prayer closet or sat in the car alone. As I advanced in my career and engaged more with the community, his jealousy only intensified. This was a burden I had borne in silence for too long.

Believing in the power of prayer, I often turned to it for solace and solutions. Yet, in doing so, I was hiding from confronting the real issues in our marriage. Prayer is vital, a direct connection to God, but it isn't a substitute for facing and addressing life's challenges head-on.

There was one incident during our marriage while we lived in Jasper when my husband, along with our pastor and his wife, arrived unannounced at our home. They revealed that he was accused of sexual harassment at work, an incident that had escalated due to flirtations with a colleague. The coworker was upset because my husband had assigned her to a position at work that she disagreed with, and as a result of not getting her way, she filed a sexual harassment complaint against him.

I was shocked and hurt. He had sought counsel from our pastors before even speaking to me about the issue. He never apologized for his actions or for bringing our pastors into our home without prior notice. In the days following, our home was enveloped in silence, a departure from my usual temperament.

The advice from our pastor's wife, suggesting that I do more to please him, felt like a misguided burden. Reluctantly, I began massaging his scalp 2-3 times per week. However, this guidance felt like another burden, an expectation to cater to his needs while mine remained unacknowledged. I followed her advice, but it left me feeling empty and unfulfilled.

Eventually, I began to pull back from these additional efforts. I questioned why I was the one making all the sacrifices when it was my husband who had jeopardized our family. His lack of remorse only compounded my pain. During a discussion about his behavior, he simply said, he just needed me to support him. This was a selfish and inconsiderate comment. How dare he ask for support when he hadn't even offered an apology?

My pastor's wife checked on our relationship and suggested he buy me a heart-shaped box of millionaire chocolates filled with nuts, a favorite of hers, as a gesture of reconciliation. However, my husband was hesitant about buying it, stating I would not accept it from him because I had not been communicating with him. She informed him that he needed to do something instead of doing nothing.

As time passed, I forgave him without receiving an apology, mainly for the sake of our family. His job was saved after the investigation, but the dynamics of our marriage had shifted.

There were moments throughout the marriage when I felt deprived. I remember exhausting myself to the point that the only time I received rest was when my body was forced to shut down which caused me to get sick.

One incident stands out from several years ago while I was on the phone with my youngest sister. That day, I had plans to meet my pastor's wife at Walgreens while my husband and sons were away heading to a football game. While talking to my sister, I suddenly felt a sharp pain in my chest and then I lost consciousness. My sister quickly contacted my youngest brother, who rushed to check on me and called 911. When the paramedics arrived, I was still unconscious, and I later regained consciousness inside the ambulance. No one in my household had noticed I was tired, and I ignored my body's warning signs, which ultimately resulted in me passing out. My body was exhausted due to a lack of sleep and not enough self-care.

I entered this marriage young, not fully prepared for all the duties it entailed. I was only twenty-one while he was twenty-nine. During the marriage, I managed to take care of four children while working. Even during times when all four children participated in sports. The house was never dirty, and I cooked at least three times per week doing what I thought was expected as wifely duties. I often found myself feeling underappreciated, a yearning that had lingered for many years. At times, all I longed for was the simple act of being remembered, hoping that someone would surprise me with a Snickers candy bar from the store. It was those small, thoughtful gestures, like remembering my favorite snacks, that meant the most.

Yet, I had poured a significant amount of time into my roles as a wife and mother, fully immersing myself in these responsibilities. When others approached me with invitations or plans, my immediate response would invariably be, "Let me check my husband's schedule or see where my children's sports activities are." I had essentially buried my own needs under the weight of these roles. I rarely had personal time except for my bi-weekly visits to the beauty shop, which were sometimes interrupted by my husband insisting the children should accompany me.

As time passed, the desire for moments of solitude grew stronger. Occasionally, I would fake illness just to savor the quietude of being alone at home. I yearned for peace, the rest, and the luxury of doing absolutely nothing. My identity had become synonymous with being a devoted wife and mother and attending church faithfully 3-4 days a week. I managed a household that included two bonus children, treating them as my own while ensuring our home was always tidy. However, balancing these responsibilities along with a full-time job gradually started to impact my physical well-being.

Regrettably, there was no time left for me. Self-care was never discussed, and I was surrounded by people who never mentioned it. I believed that fulfilling my roles was sufficient to keep my family happy, not fully grasping my own need for replenishment. In moments of solitude, tears often welled up as I silently hoped that someone would hear my unspoken cries. All I desired was acknowledgment and appreciation, whether through simple gestures like receiving a favorite snack or a small gift, especially during the holidays.

I believe my husband assumed that my contentment stemmed from not asking for much. However, even though I rarely made demands for my desires, the simple act of someone thinking of me would have been enough to bring a heartfelt smile to my face.

These events were among the many that led to our eventual divorce. Despite being a dedicated wife and mother, my needs and well-being were consistently overlooked. I had become a caretaker in every sense, yet I was the one who was emotionally and physically depleted. This realization was the catalyst for me to seek a new path, one where I could reclaim my voice.

In September 2019, the most difficult part of filing for divorce was the fact that I had three children with him. My oldest daughter had just graduated high school in May 2019. I had already postponed filing for divorce as long as I could, not wanting to disrupt her senior year. I wanted her to focus on graduating, especially since we recently moved to Lufkin the year before. By postponing, I thought I was making an unselfish decision as a mother, not realizing it was also causing me more agony.

I vividly remember the moment during my daughter's graduation celebration in May 2019 when the topic of divorce was already on the table between my husband and me. He was adamant that we were not getting a divorce. On that Saturday, which was supposed to be a celebration of my daughter's achievements, my husband informed my family that he was planning a surprise wedding vow renewal for me. He asked them not to tell me.

During the celebration, while I was in the kitchen, he managed to gather everyone inside the house for his proposal. This caught me completely off guard because I'm usually not someone who can be easily surprised. However, while in the kitchen, he knelt in front of everyone and delivered a speech about his love for me. He asked if I would consider renewing our vows and spending more years with him.

I was both angry and speechless at this stunt. I sat there, staring at him in disbelief, wondering how he could pull such a move in front of my family. I thought, "How dare you embarrass me like this? What is your purpose?" I felt humiliated, wondering if he intended to publicly embarrass me. He continued to kneel, waiting for my response, and the entire house fell silent, anticipating my answer.

Two minutes passed, and I was still staring at him in anger, refusing to give a response because I didn't want to create a scene in front of my family. They had no idea about the issues in our marriage, and I couldn't bring myself to voice my feelings. I knew that his attempt was an act of desperation, a way to prove a point to my family. This was intended to be a celebration for my daughter, and I couldn't understand why he would do this on her special day.

While everyone waited for me to respond, my eldest sister yelled out, "Girl, just say yes" as if she wanted the ordeal to end. I'm not sure how many minutes passed while everyone waited, but that incident ignited a deep anger within me. He had somehow managed to instruct my family not to tell me about his plan. I'm not sure when he eventually stood up from the floor because I never gave him a "yes." Somehow, we managed to continue with the rest of my daughter's celebration, but it left me feeling embarrassed and even more broken.

That moment was an unforgettable experience. I was like a tightly sealed soda bottle, the pressure building inside, struggling to maintain my composed exterior. I feared that if the cap were to come off, I would erupt like a shaken soda, unleashing a storm of emotions.

Months later, when I discovered he had been communicating with other women, I filed for divorce. However, after filing he refused to leave the home. So, we were living together, even though he had been served divorce papers. The situation became increasingly intense, and I tried my best to shield our children from it. However, one day, the intensity of our arguments reached a breaking point. The children heard the heated exchange from their bedroom. I attempted to leave the home to attend church that night, but he barricaded his car behind mine to prevent me from leaving. The situation escalated to the point where I had to call the police. They arrived, and he eventually moved his car, allowing me to leave for church. While I was at church, he showed up with his shirt all wrinkled, as if he had rushed to confirm my whereabouts. He sat in the back during the service, wearing an angered expression. It was a profoundly embarrassing moment for me.

Reflecting on the seventeen years of our marriage, from its beginning in January 2003 to our divorce in April 2020, I recall the journey of managing new responsibilities, adjusting to unexpected revelations, and navigating the challenges of a blended family. The constant undercurrent of my husband's jealousy and the mounting pressures of our life together gradually eroded the foundations of our union.

I must be honest; it wasn't all bad. There were moments throughout the marriage when we continued to celebrate our anniversary every year, but the cracks in our relationship were growing, hidden beneath the surface. Some cracks appear not to be that dangerous and get overlooked, but over time, they can widen and deepen, causing significant issues. We both had areas within us that needed repairs, but instead of addressing and mending those issues, they were left unattended. Our marriage began with limited knowledge about what marriage truly entailed. We lacked the guidance and examples to navigate the complexities of married life. While we had parents, friends, and a pastor who had been married for a long time, there was a noticeable absence of in-depth teachings on the intricacies of marriage. In fact, during all the years of attending my church in Jasper, we only had one marriage ministry service, leaving us ill-prepared for the challenges that lay ahead.

We knew the power of prayer, and indeed, prayer is powerful, however, some issues require more than prayer alone; they demand proper communication and deliverance to bridge the gaps in the cracks we both had.

After the divorce, I felt an excitement I had never experienced before. I busied myself with projects around the house, completing tasks that had been left unfinished. A sense of freedom flowed over me, and I no longer felt the weight of restrictions that had once held me back. It was as if a heavy burden had been lifted from my shoulders, and I had no desire to rekindle our relationship. Strangely, it seemed like all the emotions I had once held for him had vanished. I didn't harbor any hatred or ill feelings towards him. I couldn't forget that he was the father of our three children, so I respected him for that. He remained a good person, but it became clear that we were not meant for each other.

I understood that following the divorce, I would have to confront criticism from those with strong religious beliefs who would assert that divorce was not the right course of action for me.

One of the reasons I entered into this marriage stemmed from the deep desire for my daughter to have an actively present father in her life. Growing up with my father in the household, I believed that providing her with a similar family structure was the best choice. During that time, a close friend and I prayed together to seek guidance from God about whether he was the right person for me to marry. My friend assured me that if he was truly meant to be my husband, God would reveal it to me through a dream. While I was familiar with the concept of dreaming, I must admit that at the age of twenty, my understanding of God and His guidance was still in the process of development. Even though I never had a dream to confirm our marriage, I still proceeded with the wedding plans.

As the wedding plans progressed, including the purchase of my dress and other preparations, I received unexpected counsel from a woman of God. She shared with me that he was not the one I should marry. My initial reaction was mixed with shock and concern. We had already invested $500 in my dress, and the wedding was just months away. Despite these early warnings, I went through with marriage at the age of twenty-one, and soon, the distinct differences between us became evident. While opposites are often said to balance each other, in our case, it felt more like an unbalanced weight, with him relying heavily on me rather than us finding equilibrium in our relationship.

I believe anything truly destined and ordained by God can withstand even the toughest battles. So, it was clear our relationship was surviving, but not thriving. I began to recognize as the relationship persisted, and though there were numerous issues within the marriage, I must admit that God allowed me to navigate through them. However, this journey was not without its consequences. In my youth and lack of knowledge, I had to pay a price for my disobedience. While our marriage may have appeared harmonious to outsiders, I endured years of pressure, unappreciation, and a stifling silence that took a toll on my physical and emotional well-being. These struggles, I bore in silence.

While Mark 10:9 emphasizes that what God has joined together, no one should separate, it became evident that our marriage wasn't something God had truly joined. As I deepened my relationship with God over the years of our marriage, I came to understand that it was permitted by God but not necessarily His divine plan. It was a situation where God allowed our choices, much like the Israelites who wanted a king for their desires, even though God had told them they didn't need one. In response to their fleshly desires, God allowed them to have a king, but it wasn't His initial will, much like my marriage. I married him because I thought it was the right thing to do. It was my unselfish desire to ensure my daughter had her father in her life.

And so I emerged from the ashes of a marriage that, though allowed by God, was not His perfect plan for my life. This ending was not absent of pain but necessary for me to walk in God's true purpose. I have gained the courage to go against the norm when required, but only when aligned with God's will. We should never fear bucking expectations to follow our compass. However, that compass must be calibrated to His true North.

Though much time was lost that can never be restored, the heat of those trials has served to refine and purify my faith. I am reminded that when metal is heated, the impurities rise to the surface to be skimmed away, revealing the precious metal lying dormant underneath. My identity has been stripped down to the studs and beams. Now is my chance to rebuild according to God's blueprint - a design anchored not in others' expectations, but the woman God created me to become.

Just as forest fires carve out the space for new life to bloom even more vibrant, I am expectant for God's new work He wants to establish within me and through me. When we walk through the valley clinging to His promises, we emerge transformed on mountain peaks to sing renewed songs of praise. My journey continues. Now, wisdom has become my trusted guide on this journey, and it has profoundly changed everything.

Chapter 5

Bridges Burned By God

Yet indeed I also count all things loss for the excellence of the knowledge of Christ Jesus my Lord, for whom I have suffered the loss of all things, and count them as rubbish, that I may gain Christ -Philippians NKJV

Reflecting on 2017 and 2018, these years were a challenging yet transformative time in my spiritual journey. They were filled with trials in my ministry and important lessons. During this period, I faced complex situations in both my role in the ministry and my personal relationships, especially with the pastor's wife and my close friend who's closely connected to her.

Pastors typically value those who are unwaveringly faithful. These individuals consistently attend services, contribute regularly, and embody their faith so genuinely that they seldom require guidance. They are the ministry's steadfast supporters, the ones you can count on without a second thought. Ordinarily, a church would do anything to retain such people. However, my story was not the typical one.

My family and I were among these devoted members. We were a vital part of the church, always present, faithful tithers, always ready to assist, never needing a reminder or a call. It was perplexing why a ministry wouldn't value and appreciate those qualities.

The change began in 2017 when the ministry started to experience subtle shifts. The pastor's wife, who was also the co-pastor, began to behave differently which affected our once close relationship. This change was also reflected in the behavior of my long-time friend, marking a key turning point in my journey with the ministry. These changes led to important decisions about my future in the ministry.

The more the church seemed to oppose us, the deeper I delved into scripture, searching for wisdom and understanding. During this time, God was teaching me about leadership – what to avoid, and what to expect. At that moment, I didn't realize that I would soon be leading a ministry myself in the future. God wanted me to grasp the principles of good ministry, as highlighted in scriptures like 1 Timothy 5:17, which advises, "The elders who direct the affairs of the church well are worthy of double honor, especially those whose work is preaching and teaching." This period was a formative lesson in leadership, emphasizing the importance of treating others well and being a leader.

This period was not only a time of facing trials but also an opportunity to gain a deeper understanding of leadership and the role of friendship in my spiritual journey. My friend, the matron of honor at my wedding, and I have shared nearly twenty years of friendship. She was also the person who introduced me to the ministry. However, our relationship began to change in unexpected ways. At the same time, I was having dreams that helped me understand these changes.

Our phone conversations, which happened at least twice a month often lasted one to two hours. It was a time for me to share my thoughts while she listened patiently. She was more than just a listener; she was a true friend who supported me in prayer, and we shared secrets with each other. We found a strong sense of comfort in each other's company. She was the youth Sunday school teacher at our church and, like many of my friends, was much older than me. I've often connected more with people older than myself.

However, I started noticing a shift in our friendship. It became distant, contrasting with our usually close bond. This change was noticeable. Around the same time, I had a significant dream, which I shared with her. I knew she would understand the dream importance, as she was the one who had encouraged me to journal my dreams many years ago by purchasing a journal for me to document them.

In the dream, I found myself at our church, standing in front of the congregation and speaking. My friend was sitting in her usual seat. As I started to speak, she stood up, showing a look of disagreement, a type of behavior I had never seen of her before. The pastor's wife, who was sitting to my friend's right, called out her name. My friend glanced towards the pastor's wife and then gave me a harsh look. Although the pastor's wife tried to calm her, she also appeared to be somewhat amused by the confrontation, smirking as if she found the situation pleasing. This dream suggested an impending conflict, where the pastor's wife would make false accusations against me, and my long-time friend would side with her.

Following this dream, the dynamics of my conversations with my friend noticeably changed. The conversations with my friend became less frequent. Our usual talks after church diminished, and it felt as if she was avoiding me. I remember calling her one day, concerned by our lack of communication and wanting to get a clear understanding of the disconnect in our friendship. The conversation was far from pleasant, unlike our usual interactions. Each question I asked her was met with sarcasm. When I reminded her of the dream I had about her and me, her response was dismissively sarcastic, 'Has it happened yet?' It was as if all of a sudden she doubted the validity of my dreams, which often came to pass. The call, which would typically last for hours, ended abruptly.

At that moment, I realized our relationship had taken its turn and would never be the same again. I hung up the phone, knowing I wouldn't call her again. Her tone and demeanor towards me had changed drastically. After nearly twenty years of close friendship, I was deeply troubled that we seemed unable to communicate openly anymore. I tried hard to understand what could have broken our friendship. As much as I wanted to restore the closeness we once shared, at a certain point I had to accept that the relationship had profoundly changed despite my best efforts. Though painful, I realized I had done nothing intentionally to damage our connection. With much sorrow, I came to the difficult conclusion that I had to let the friendship go, even knowing that meant losing someone so meaningful who had been a treasured part of my life for so long. What had happened to this long-time friend, my confidante, who was always ready to assist me? Was her loyalty to the pastor's wife the reason for this distance?

My relationship with the pastor's wife had also changed. We were once close, with her interpreting my dreams and providing guidance. I noticed her behavior towards me changed notably as I took on a more prominent role in preaching and prophesying. I preached every third Sunday, which was youth Sunday, and she rarely attended on those days. When she did attend, she often ignored my teachings by chatting with others while I preached, which I perceived as disrespectful. However, I tried to overlook it most of the time, focusing on delivering the Word of God.

Interestingly, more people showed up on those third Sundays eager to hear me preach including my friend's husband who rarely attended services.

An elderly man from a nursing home, whom our church often brought to services, usually sat quietly with his head down. But on the Sundays I preached, he would listen attentively and smile, a noticeable change from his usual demeanor. After the services, he would often compliment my teaching, which always brought a smile to my face.

As my relationship with the pastor's wife deteriorated, I observed notable changes in her behavior. I would usually approach her for a hug after the service, but she started walking away as I approached, a noticeable and frequent change from her usual behavior of remaining seated after services. Our phone calls also became less frequent. As these events unfolded, I found myself reflecting deeply on the meaning of my spiritual journey.

On one third Sunday, while I was releasing a prophetic message to a visitor, my pastor interrupted me to allow his wife to make an announcement. I can't recall what the announcement was, but it felt trivial and disruptive. The visitor's expression at that moment was unforgettable.

Following this, the pastor's wife became increasingly distant. Another incident highlighted this during our summer vacation Bible school, which I had organized annually, often investing a lot of my own money. The church typically contributed a small budget, usually less than $100, for snacks, supplies, activities, and decorations over five days. However, I would personally add at least $200 each year. Due to financial limits, I had to reduce the Bible school to three days the following year.

Despite my significant contributions, I sensed a lack of appreciation for my efforts. It often felt like my hard work and generosity were misinterpreted as arrogance.

The classes were set up to have two teachers per group, but due to budget constraints, I could only provide supplies for the main teacher.

One day, the pastor's wife confronted me while two of her daughters were present, demanding that I buy more tote bags filled with supplies so that both teachers in each class could have them, despite these supplies did not come from the church's budget.

Furthermore, I recall a summer when my efforts in organizing the vacation Bible school went unrecognized. Although I never complained about how I felt I believed that I deserved some type of appreciation even if it was a small gesture. This oversight was even noted by the Deacon. The following summer, after the Deacon spoke to the leadership, they acknowledged my contributions with a gift - a purse I suspected was a re-gift from the pastor's wife. It was not the fact that I was looking for special recognition or demanded it, but the way the matter was handled toward me was hurtful and undeserving.

My concerns about her changing behavior towards me deepened. We had never disagreed, and I held her in high regard as the pastor's wife. I even contributed money from my paycheck every two weeks as a love offering to her. Looking back, her expressions of thanks were rare; she often exclaimed 'glory' or 'glory hallelujah' for significant amounts, but seldom uttered words of appreciation.

In one incident during a phone conversation, she accused me of gossiping to former church members about her, claiming God revealed this to her. I knew this wasn't true; these accusations stemmed from her own emotions and past issues with those members. I was never one to gossip or start trouble, and I realized the enemy was deceiving her thoughts. As the scripture says, satan is the accuser, and a spirit at that moment was using her with false accusations.

I felt if there were any issues with my behavior or ministerial role, the pastor and his wife should have discussed them with me. This lack of communication was a missed opportunity for resolution and growth. As a leader, I firmly believe in addressing issues directly through conversation. The absence of such dialogue suggested that my conduct was not the problem, but rather it was their unfounded beliefs without evidence.

The tension in our relationship escalated. On one occasion, I arrived late to teach adult Sunday School, a class she rarely attended. That day, she was there, seated at the back near the entrance, as if anticipating my arrival. When I entered, she confronted me, asking if I had a problem with her. Surprised but composed, I denied the false accusations. She then warned me that if I had a problem with her then I needed to remove myself from sitting in the pulpit. Her approach seemed designed to provoke an argument, but I chose not to engage and walked away, focusing on maintaining a positive spirit for teaching. This interaction seemed intentional as if she wanted to provoke me into leaving the church, which has occurred on other occasions with past believers who once attended the ministry. Yet, I stayed, believing in the blessing of humility as described in Matthew 5:5 – 'Blessed are the meek, for they shall inherit the earth.'

Although I'm usually not one to shy away from confrontation, I had respect for her and believed that responding would only escalate the situation. It was as if God was silencing me. We were taught not to argue with elders. The scripture my pastor and his wife often quoted, 'Do not rebuke an elder,' felt like it was used more to intimidate or allow elders to speak freely without expecting a response. This perspective on scripture highlighted the imbalance of power and the misuse of scripture to silence disagreement.

The tension in our relationship grew further. On another third Sunday, I went to my car during the service to retrieve something I had forgotten. There, I was met by the pastor's wife, who informed me that I would not be preaching that day because a visitor, supposedly the pastor's classmate, was present. Her words immediately confirmed a feeling I had earlier that morning and I had texted my husband, sensing I would not be ministering that day. After she said those words, I began to pray, to which she inquired why I was praying like that. When I responded that God had already spoken to me, she walked away abruptly.

This interaction left me deeply disturbed. I realized that her intention was not to allow the pastor to preach, but rather, she did not want to hear me preach that Sunday.

As I re-entered the church, the choir was beginning to sing. Standing at the front with others, I struggled to focus, still disturbed by our interaction. She watched me intently as I stood there. Many might have thought I was singing by the movement of my lips, but I was praying, disturbed by her motives. The visitor, who was supposedly the pastor's classmate, left before the sermon. When this happened, I glanced at the pastor's wife, who had a blank expression on her face. This event confirmed her desire to silence my voice in the ministry.

Later, during a call with my friend, I mentioned this incident, and she informed me that the visitor was not the pastor's classmate. It became evident that the pastor's wife did not want to hear me preach on that Sunday. Her actions were part of a manipulative and deceptive plot. This realization, especially considering her frequent absence on youth Sundays, revealed the depth of the underlying issues she had toward me.

Over time, the pastor's wife continued with subtle actions that might have gone unnoticed by some, but I discerned her intentions. My habit of walking barefoot in comfortable places, like the church, was criticized by her as showing off my feet. My natural hand movements while speaking, a part of my expressive personality, were also condemned. She accused me of trying to show off my long nails. Her scrutiny seemed to be a search for justifications for her feelings. Her behavior later became apparent to many, including children, yet no one spoke up.

During my time in the ministry, there were moments when the pastor's wife accused me of intentionally studying her husband's, wardrobe because we often coincidently wore matching colors. The idea of intentionally dressing like him was absurd to me. I respected him as my spiritual leader and had no such intentions. The coincidental matching of our outfits, which I saw as a spiritual alignment, was misinterpreted as a deliberate action. This misunderstanding highlighted her struggle with deeper issues, possibly needing intervention and deliverance.

In response to these growing tensions, I stopped answering her calls, suspecting they were part of her manipulative tactics.

Then one night in a dream God began to give me further warnings regarding her behavior. I then shared this dream with my friend. In this dream, my husband and I were about to purchase a new truck. In the dream, others were admiring it, but the pastor's wife stood far off, looking on in disgust. Later this dream confirmed a real event that occurred after my husband bought the truck. The church's stance was that "members" would need to consult with the pastor's wife before making significant life changes, like buying a home or a car, or other things to ensure it was God's Will.

When my husband and I purchased that truck, it was something we did not do.

Later, I realized how controlling this was, a manifestation of a 'Jezebel spirit'. Everything had to be screened by her, every idea, every decision. This action held many back from reaching their full potential.

Despite the hurt caused by her actions, God spoke to me in March 2018, promising that if I kept my hands clean and heart pure, He would "bring it to naught." This meant that if I didn't retaliate and remained humble, He would handle the situation and not allow her plots to prosper against me.

Holding on to this Word with faith in God, I began to navigate the situation. I kept these issues only between my husband and me, striving to maintain peace.

I learned that in God, it's not about seniority anointing, but about humility in the face of opposition. This lesson became a guiding principle, helping me to find meaning in these challenges. As I pondered the nature of these attacks, I questioned whether they were intended to push me out of my comfort zone, prompting me to seek new spiritual horizons.

As tensions escalated, I strived to find meaning rather than taking her behavior personally. While our routine faithfulness had cultivated obedience, I felt increasingly starved for revelation and new challenges to awaken new gifts stirring within me. Part of me sensed a deeper purpose - that it was time for a necessary shift out of complacency so I could grow into new callings. I questioned, "Were these attacks meant to push me from my comfort zone?"

It reminded me of the scriptures in I Samuel chapters 18, 19, and 20, where David, who once had a close relationship with King Saul, became his enemy. David began to avoid Saul when he realized Saul was trying to target and kill him. Similarly, while she may not have been trying to kill me physically her actions towards me demonstrated hostility and killed the once close relationship we had.

As 2018 approached, things grew more intense. My husband and I, now residing in a different city, continued our commitment to the church, driving sixty miles every Sunday for nine months. Despite my dedication, I had never been officially ordained, even after fifteen years of association and nearly nine years of serving as a minister.

During a meeting, our pastor mentioned the possibility of granting us ministry licenses, initially temporary, followed by permanent ones six months later. Unfamiliar with the licensing process, I initially believed this proposition, although I sensed it was a tactic to keep us tied to the ministry.

While reflecting on our roles and the ministry's path, we encountered an unexpected event that deepened our doubts about the honesty and integrity of our church's leaders. During this time, my husband, who often confided in the pastor, found his calls going unanswered. Sensing something was wrong, I suggested he try calling from a different phone number. After doing this the call went through, revealing that his original number had been blocked on the pastor's phone. The pastor who's not tech-savvy, was unaware of this and we suspected his wife's involvement. Although not certain, her behavior led us to conclude she might be responsible. We believed either she or someone she instructed had blocked the number to force my husband to call their house instead. This would ensure she would be aware of their phone calls to monitor the conversations.

This period was challenging, but revealing, showing the true nature of our church's leadership and the spiritual journey we were navigating. Despite the challenges, we continued to love and respect our pastors and remained loyal to the ministry, just as we had before.

I began yearning more for fresh insights to awaken dormant talents within me, sensing a need to break free from my comfort zone and embrace new callings. The desire for new revelations grew, reflecting the changes around me. However, seeking answers outside our usual teachings was seen as foolish and or rebellious by our pastors. I knew something important was happening within me because it was evident what was happening around me.

On one Sunday in November 2018, as we were driving about twenty-five of our sixty-mile journey to church services, a pivotal moment unfolded. It was the third Sunday and my day to preach, but something shifted in our spirits. In an immediate unplanned turn, we chose not to return to the ministry to where I had dedicated fifteen years of my life. It marked the end of one chapter and the beginning of another. My husband called our pastor to inform him of our decision not to return. We had hoped for a response that acknowledged our years of faithful service and the significant contributions we had made, working closely with our leaders, and heading many auxiliaries. But there were no blessings, no words of gratitude. Instead, his response was, 'We kinda figured y'all would eventually leave since you moved.'

My husband detected disappointment in our pastor's voice. At that moment, I felt God fulfilling His promise to me. He allowed me to leave in peace, without causing any uproar or having my name tarnished, which I had feared was the intent of my pastor's wife. I'm unsure why we chose that particular day not to return, especially since it was my usual day to preach, but I remained confident that the decision served a purpose.

Departures from the ministry were often met with negativity, especially from the pastor's wife, who would say, 'every time someone leaves the church, something bad happens to them.' However, we left with our dignity intact, a testament to God's protection and the power of faith in challenging times. This experience reinforced the belief that some battles don't need to be fought with words or actions; sometimes, allowing God to work is the most profound statement of faith.

Our decision to leave the ministry in November 2018 left me wondering about their thoughts on our departure. Despite the challenges, including losing a long-term friendship and enduring attacks, we were ready to move forward. This decision embodied Philippians 3:14, pressing on toward our spiritual goal, undeterred by the trials we faced.

I believe God burned that bridge. When I reflect on the concept of a burned bridge, it emerges as a touching metaphor. To burn a bridge is to sever a pathway, a connection that once linked two points. In the context of relationships, it symbolizes the end of a bond. However, a burned bridge does not necessarily mean you harbor ill feelings or no longer care for that person. Nor does it imply unforgiveness or hatred. Rather, it simply signifies that the closeness and ease of interaction have been lost. The link between others still exists in memory and history, but the bridge itself can no longer be crossed.

Once that bridge is burned, it's not just the connection that's lost, but also the closeness and ease of interaction that it facilitated. I learned that sometimes, God burns bridges in our lives. In my case, it was to teach me invaluable lessons about leadership, guide me toward understanding the best practices of ministry, and prepare me for the future.

Our family's journey in this ministry was significant. My children grew up there, it's where my daughter was baptized, and my son was christened in that church. It was where I first trained as a minister and where I first received the Holy Ghost. My early experiences of revivals and learning about prophecy happened in this church. We began our first involvement by cleaning the church and learning the foundations of prayer, fasting, and sowing. Our involvement was extensive, from financial contributions to leading various ministries. In the fifteen years of my association, only once did my family need resources from the church, which we promptly repaid, signifying we gave more than we took. My roles were varied, including coordinating Vacation Bible School, teaching adult Sunday School, and assisting in the Women's Ministry. Many of the prophetic words I heard there are now coming true in my life, serving as evidence of the profound spiritual foundation laid during those transformative years.

As I pressed on toward my spiritual goal, undeterred by the trials I faced, the journey taught me the value of understanding my purpose, remaining steadfast in the face of adversity, and the power of humility. I understood that leaving the ministry was not the same as leaving God; my foundation was still solid. This departure from a place that had imparted valuable lessons about prayer, fasting, and consecration marked a necessary step in my spiritual evolution. God kept His promise to me as I kept my promise to Him, allowing me to leave there in peace with my hands clean and heart pure.

After approximately two months of searching for another ministry, we remained faithful in paying our tithes, saving them until we found the right place. During one of our visits to a ministry while in Lufkin, my husband surprised me by deciding to join during the service we attended. Despite my initial surprise, I quickly followed his lead.

As my journey continued, each trial and revelation became a testament to God's faithfulness. From the challenges of departing from familiar ground to the unexpected decision made by my husband, I remained faithful in trusting God's plan. With my heart open to His guidance, I embraced each step forward, knowing that His promises would be fulfilled as I remained dedicated to my calling in Christ.

Chapter 6

Adjusting to the Heat

When thou passest through the waters, I will be with thee; and through the rivers, they shall not overflow thee: when thou walkest through the fire, thou shalt not be burned; neither shall the flame kindle upon thee.

-Isaiah 43:2

In 2021, a year filled with new beginnings, my life took many unexpected turns. I did not realize this year would mark the beginning of many firsts in my journey.

While residing in Lufkin, Texas it all began with a phone conversation with a pastor from Lafayette, Louisiana. I shared with him my deep sense of urgency to make a move, even though I couldn't fully comprehend the reasons behind it. His response was,

"If God wants you to move, He will make a way." I shared this urgency with my Overseer in Baton Rouge, hoping for some affirmation. However, her reaction was not what I expected. Her response was, "Oh, Lord," and she then quickly changed the topic of our conversation. Despite the lack of support, I knew that when God placed something in my spirit, nothing could deter me.

At this point, I wasn't sure about the where and when of this move, but I felt it deep within. A month later, I had a dream. In it, I found myself in a real estate sale, selling off all my furniture possessions. I shared this vision with my two sons, but they were hesitant, we had only lived in Lufkin for only three years. They were in the 10th and 12th grades and had no desire to move again.

Then, on one Friday, August 6th, while I was at work conducting a loan signing, I received a call from my youngest son. I knew something was wrong because he was aware that I was at work, so I knew the call was an important one. He nervously explained that someone had entered our home, opened the living room door, and left. I thought it couldn't have been my ex-husband, their father, and the only other possibility was the landlord. Upon contacting the owner, I learned that he had made the decision to sell the house, and I had just thirty days to vacate. I was in shock, realizing that what I had felt in my spirit and the dream about the real estate sale was accurate.

Later when I came home, I remembered the check that I wrote for the rent was still lying on the shelf in my living room. I had not mailed the check for August rent, and it wasn't something that occurred often. I began to think about all those times I kept forgetting to mail the check, I understood now it was for a reason. During the phone conversation with the landlord, he stated that I did not have to pay for rent in August. So that check was sitting there as a divine plan of God.

I then began to immediately say to myself, "How can I move and run my business at the same time? I need to work." Having lived in Lufkin for just three years without family, my connections were limited to a few church acquaintances and my ex-husband.

I owned a notary and tax business that I had recently launched in October 2020, which was less than one year old making it my primary source of income. That very week, all my scheduled loan signings were canceled and I received texts and emails from the signing companies informing me of the cancellations. I missed over one thousand dollars for that one week. I understood God was sending me a clear message, "You said you couldn't move and work simultaneously, so I've removed your work commitments." God has a way of canceling our will for His. Now that God removed the excuse, I had to prepare for the move.

Throughout the entire month of August, I had no signings, not even with the company where I was the preferred notary. I endured a month without income.

I also operated a customized shirt business out of my garage, and I had to turn down large orders to prepare for the move. Again, no income.

It's important to understand that I had left my corporate job a year prior in December 2020 out of obedience to God. A position where I was making nearly thirty dollars per hour and my notary and tax business hadn't yet reached that level of income replacement.

I explained to my two sons that we had to move, and they were understandably upset. In 2018, we moved to Lufkin, followed by my divorce from their father in 2020. Now, I was telling them that we had to move again. They expressed their unwillingness to move or stay with their father. Given the uncertainty of my living situation, I had no choice but to suggest that they stay with their dad temporarily while I searched for a new place. I then began to search for a new residence.

I reached out to some local realtors in Lufkin to search for a house, but it seemed that no one had any listings available. Turning to the Facebook Marketplace, I found an area but realized the owner had removed his contact info. I applied for several properties but found myself on long waiting lists.

Staying in run-down, cheap apartments wasn't an option for me, especially with two sons to consider. I was struggling to find a safe, decent place to live, and time was running out. Every place I went to was not available or resulted in a no.

I began to pray and ask God for a strategy because I wasn't sure where to go or what to do. Shortly after, God gave me a dream about where I needed to relocate. In the dream, I was having a conversation with my youngest sister about a storm approaching Louisiana and my need to return to Texas because I lacked furniture. The place where I was living in the dream resembled a two-story, beautiful building, like an apartment with half-brick and half-siding. It was situated in a gated community. This dream prompted me to call an apostle in South Africa, who insisted that I must move to Louisiana. He stated to me, "Woman of God, that dream is too detailed. You must move!" I was reluctant. I did not want to move to Louisiana, an area known for its storms. Still, I knew I had to obey God, who hadn't specified a particular city in the dream but urged me to embark on the journey to Louisiana.

With no income and no other options, I decided to begin the process of moving. I spent over one thousand dollars on a U-Haul and storage units. I realized that I had to go to Louisiana to find my exact destination, as God had shut down my resources and left me with no excuses. I put the rest of my belongings in storage and sold my furniture, washer, dryer, and refrigerator - all of which were in excellent condition because they were just purchased three years prior when we moved to Lufkin. I even sold lawnmowers, picnic tables, and items from my garage. It was now September, and my parents came to help me with the remainder of the move. Now it was time to make the move to Louisiana.

I reached out to a male acquaintance I knew who lived in Louisiana and shared with him some of my situation. We will identify him as Mr. Rayes. He allowed me to stay with him temporarily, though his cousin, a traveling nurse, also lived there. I made my journey to Louisiana, leaving behind my two sons with their father. As a mother, leaving my children behind was saddening, but it was a decision I had prayed about, and God permitted me. I was concerned about the potential changes in their spiritual upbringing as they would now be living with their father, who wouldn't provide the same church involvement and Bible study that they were accustomed to with me. However, I tried to reassure myself they were boys who needed their father's male presence. There were moments when I cried because I felt as if I had abandoned my boys.

Before I made my way to Louisiana, I contacted the pastor in Lafayette and expressed my concerns about living in the same house with a single man. He advised me that he believed I would be okay. I did have some concerns about people's perceptions if others were to find out. Additionally, I also knew I had to be cautious to avoid any temptations with Mr. Rayes while temporarily staying there.

I made plans to spend my days away from the house, exploring parks, malls, and various places to pass the time on the days he was at home. This was a deliberate strategy to minimize our time together. At night, I returned, determined to maintain a platonic relationship. I deliberately kept my appearance modest to avoid any potential enticements.

There were times when we did go eat at restaurants, but I clearly stated to him that we would have no relationship and my situation was temporary. He agreed as if he understood.

I wore large baggy pajamas and only sprayed my perfumes when I was outside the house or on days that I knew he had to work long hours. This was because I was careful not to entice him sexually with my perfume scents. Trying to ensure that I continued not to entice him became exhausting and it seemed as if it was another job. It was a constant effort that left me feeling uncomfortable.

While there I began to minister to him. I noticed the more I gave him advice about his situation and the more I encouraged him to develop a relationship with God, the more he desired me. I was uncertain about what to do, so I did what I knew, to pray because I had no desire to be with this man.

While there I realized God was doing something. I was in a place of solitude, away from familiar faces and many did not know my location.

My mom called me one day on speaker with my dad in the background. They were concerned because it had been a few days since they had heard from me. Their concern was understandable as this was not typical behavior for me. During the phone call, mom asked me where I was staying and I responded to her, "When God wants me to release it, I will let you know." This response seemed to suffice for the moment, as my mom and dad did not press it further.

During my stay in Louisiana, I understood that God was at work. He was providing me with a chance to rest, something I hadn't experienced before. Being away from everyone was a new experience for me. My children didn't know my exact whereabouts; all they knew was their mom was in Louisiana. For the first time, I slept longer than usual. I didn't realize how extremely tired my body was. I had been existing off what had felt like "fumes." My body had been exhausted for years.

I never forgot the words God spoke to me while there, saying, "rest." These words were unusual for me to hear, given my personality. I was always active and constantly supporting others. The last two decades of my life had been dedicated to being a wife, mother, and servant of God. No one ever told me to rest. I was always told to keep going. Stopping was considered giving up. I was accustomed to activity and being involved. However, at this moment I was placed in a situation where I had no choice but to rest.

Since I was now able to rest more, I began to feel the difference in my strength. Mr. Rayes was attentive, ensuring I had food and ate. Whatever I desired to eat no matter the cost, he paid for it. Additionally, when his cousin was home from work, she generously paid for our trips to get manicures and pedicures. They both said my presence brought a peaceful and pleasant feeling, so buying things for me was their modest way of reciprocating.

Yet I still struggled with the concept of resting. Part of me enjoyed it, while another part was accustomed to being active. I felt as if I needed to do something. My independent nature felt as if I was relying too much on others. However, God was orchestrating this season to gently humble my self-reliance. To find a balance I decided to contribute by paying the electricity bill every month, a small gesture to ensure I didn't feel like I was freeloading. Through it all, my lifelong sense of independence was being humbled. This experience taught me to accept help and to let go of my pride.

As an independent woman relying on someone else for a temporary place to stay was challenging for me. Deep down I sensed God orchestrating a spiritual pruning, using my circumstances to peel back the layers of pride in my self-sufficiency.

An aspect of humility involves acknowledging the need for assistance from others and recognizing one's limitations. In this situation, where I was stripped of my normal resources, and my control and options were limited, God was cultivating a healthy sense of dependency.

Through small gestures, like insisting on contributing financially even when not expected to, I resisted complete surrender. Relying daily on another for shelter was working to soften my stubbornness. Throughout this time, the Spirit worked within me not to condemn, but to heal and guide my independent spirit towards embracing the interdependence found in God's plan. As seasons changed, I was slowly learning to find freedom and power in humility.

As I navigated my journey of personal growth and humility, I noticed a shift in Mr. Rayes' behavior. While I continued to offer him advice and support, his feelings towards me were intensified, despite my non-reciprocal stance. Aware of this shift, I relied on prayer for guidance.

On a Thursday evening, on September 23, I was using my computer in the living room when he entered, freshly showered, and wearing cologne. He sat on the opposite couch and asked me to extend my hand. Confused, I questioned his request. He asked again, and as I held out my hand, he produced a diamond ring. Shocked, I withdrew my hand and questioned his intentions. Despite my previous clarity that our relationship was to be purely platonic, he expressed his desire not to 'pass up a woman like me.' I firmly reiterated that we were not compatible and that he was not the man I was destined to be with. Disturbed by the encounter, I walked to the bedroom and closed the door.

This incident echoed a dream I had on May 5, 2021. In the dream, a man offered me a ring, which I refused. Then, in the dream, my true husband appeared with a unique ring adorned with greenery flowers. The recent situation with Mr. Rayes closely resembled this dream, leading me to believe that the rest of the dream, involving my future husband, would soon manifest.

This similarity between the dream and the incident was not just a coincidence, but a divine orchestration. That dream, seemingly prophetic, involved a similar scenario where Mr. Rayes' proposal was met with my refusal. This was not merely a rejection of the proposal, but a reaffirmation of my faith in God's greater plan. What followed in the dream was the emergence of my true husband, symbolic of the right path and divine timing, as stated in the message found in Ecclesiastes 3:1 about seasons and purposes. It was a powerful reminder that life's unexpected turns can be part of a larger narrative, one that is guided by faith and a deeper understanding of my journey toward destiny.

Mr. Rayes' desire for me led to a lack of respect for my faith and values. He wanted me - the woman I am and the divine presence I carried. My being there seemed to taunt him. He could not comprehend how I could live under the same roof yet not reciprocate his physical desires. This, I believe, fueled his frustration and anger. He tried to belittle me, insinuating that I considered myself superior. But his condescending remarks didn't affect me; my self-worth and identity in Christ remained intact.

He did not understand that it was my faith keeping me grounded. Yes, I am a woman with natural desires. I haven't forgotten the feeling of a man's touch. My last intimate moment with my husband was in 2019, before our divorce in 2020. Then, two years later, I experienced a regrettable moment of weakness with another man in early 2021. The aftermath of that encounter left me determined not to repeat such a mistake because it took some time for me to recover from the emotional impact it had on me.

I did not want to put myself in such a position again, nor delay my destined covenant husband from finding me one day. Though the temptation arose, I exerted great effort to remain chaste - for I only desired to give that gift to the future partner God had planned for me. Giving in to Mr. Rayes would not just be a sin - it would likely drive his desire for me further while taking me off the righteous path. That was too heavy a chance for me to take.

Then things began to take a further turn. One night while in the bedroom where I was sleeping, God instructed me to pray. I then immediately woke up and began to pray. While I was kneeling on the bed praying, he entered the bedroom without knocking and opened the door. He saw me praying and then shut the door. During that moment, I knew the reason God wanted me to pray. The prayer at that moment shifted the atmosphere. I don't know what exactly would have taken place, but I believe he entered that bedroom desiring to have sex with me, but prayer halted his plans.

Days after, he tried various tactics to gain my attention, which I consistently ignored. His behavior ranged from intentional mean actions due to my rejection. He then began flaunting his money to attract me. Each of these actions made me increasingly uncomfortable.

One evening while he, his cousin, and I were sitting in the living room, he began counting his money in front of me. I knew it was a way to entice me. So, I decided to leave the room. Several weeks later he repeated this same behavior. At this time, I am getting upset because now it seems like he was insulting me. So, I began to pray, and I said, "Lord if he does this to me one more time, I am going to snatch this money, rip and tear it, and throw it in the trash because he is disrespecting me." The warrior in me wanted to stand up, but I knew if I did this, things could get dangerous.

God knew my temper and God knew I was serious. I knew that things could escalate dangerously if I stepped outside of God's Will in this situation. God was fully aware of my temperament and knew I meant what I said. Thankfully, Mr. Rayes never propositioned me in that way again after seeing I stood firm. Still, I made a point to inform him that money will not persuade or sway me to do things against the will of God - I am a woman of integrity who knows how to work hard and build security for myself.

As time progressed, Mr. Rayes began to have company over. Whenever he had his female friends or family over, I had to find another place to stay. On this day I decided to take a drive to Lafayette looking at houses and commercial buildings in Carencro, Louisiana. While I was there, God was speaking to me. God began to reveal to me the business He was going to bless me with, however, I was very emotional that day. My thoughts were consumed with being in an area without family, and the fact I had to start over in ministry because only a few people knew me there. I drove to Lafayette that night and while I did not have a place to stay, I slept in my car in the parking lot. I cried continually. As a woman of faith, I couldn't understand why I had to endure these circumstances. It felt as though God owed me better for simply fulfilling my calling. This was foolish and emotional thinking.

God normally would give me more direction, but this chapter of my life seemed as if He was giving me portions of the divine plan.

That night I slept in the parking lot in my car, reclining my seat back with my .380 automatic caliber pistol in my lap, not knowing what to expect. I was mentally exhausted that day as if I had done physical labor. With my gun in my lap, I prayed, then leaned my head back, and a deep sleep fell upon me. I woke up the next morning and drove to Rayes' apartment to bathe and then I left. He would routinely have friends or family who stayed over so I stayed in hotels and slept in my car. Although not many knew, I was essentially homeless, sleeping in my car, while I was also doing Facebook Lives. This continued for a period of three months.

Some would say that it was foolishness, that I could have contacted friends or family for a place to stay. However, I was committed to following God's directive to be in Louisiana. Any other place would have been interfering in the plan of God, and I did not want to risk anyone having to endure the wrath of God for interfering in His plans. I wanted a way to escape, but I knew obedience was more important. This obedience came at a cost: I lost my house, my independence, and I am now living with another man and sometimes sleeping in my car. This was a blow to my pride and independence, but in my faith, I understood that God was teaching me something. I reminded myself of the words I quoted often, "God will never take you through without blessing you," as a reminder to hold on to faith.

As I navigated this season of homelessness and uncertainty, I couldn't help but reflect on the biblical verses of those who also stepped out in faith. Consider Abraham, who demonstrated complete trust even when commanded to sacrifice his promised son Isaac (Genesis 22:1-18). Or the Israelites, who relied on pillars of clouds and fire to guide them blindly towards a land they had not seen (Exodus 13:21-22). For me, this transition held deep spiritual meaning, reminiscent of the disciples who followed Jesus without fully knowing where He was leading them (Matthew 4:18-22).

As I reflected, I recognized God's pattern of testing obedience through the unknown. Now I'm no Abraham, but the Lord consistently examines our faith, whether on Mount Moriah or the streets of Louisiana. I couldn't choose to run like Jonah then I would face the consequences of being overtaken for disobedience (Jonah 1-2). Nor could I persist in stubbornness like Balaam, by going to Moab against God's warning. Then God had to forcibly intervene for Balaam to open his eyes to go in the right direction (Numbers 22:21-34). These accounts remind us to trust in the Lord with all our hearts rather than our limited logic (Proverbs 3:5). When God orders us to "move," we must respond accordingly, anchored by faith that His perfect plan is at work.

As the events of the first part of 2021 came to a close, I realized how much my life had changed. I had faced many challenges and had grown from them. However, as I reached this point, I knew more was about to unfold. The next part of my story was about to begin, filled with even more challenges and deeper insights into my life and faith.

Chapter 7

Surviving The Heat

See, I have refined you, though not as silver;
I have tested you in the furnace of affliction. - Isaiah 48:10

ntering the second half of 2021, I braced myself for what was yet to come. This next chapter was about to bring new challenges and deeper emotional experiences, particularly with my family. I was ready to learn and grow from these upcoming events, holding onto my faith as I moved forward.

Throughout these changes, God continued to communicate with me through dreams and visions, revealing to me the usual secret intel.

In June, I experienced a vivid dream about a family funeral. I found myself in a funeral home, where I walked in to see my family gathered. Among them, the faces of my two oldest sisters were distinct, each seated on opposite sides of a pew. As I entered, I overheard and interrupted a conversation about me. At the front of the church, there was a casket, but the face of the person inside it remained concealed from me. This dream carried a divine warning of potential family division stemming from this funeral. A few days later, I shared this dream with my siblings via text.

In July 2021, I felt God leading me to speak with my parents about their burial arrangements. I contacted my parents and my mom provided clear instructions about their burial desires. A few days later, my dad called me to designate two of my siblings as power of attorney in case any issues would occur while they were alive. I relayed this information to my siblings in a group text.

In August 2021, my parents attended one of my worship services, unknowingly for the last time. That same month, a prophet from New Orleans, Louisiana, gave me a prophecy about my mom, speaking of her in the past tense. I didn't break down the revelation from the prophecy's meaning at the time but later understood that he was speaking from the spirit, of how my mom would die months later.

In September 2021, a week before my parents fell ill, God gave me another vision. In it, I dreamt of remarrying and tearfully explaining to my spouse how my mom would have loved him. I spoke of her in the past tense, as if she were already gone. This dream stirred deep emotions within me, revealing the impending loss I was about to face. That same month, my parents both became sick. Also in September 2021, just before falling ill, my parents traveled to Lufkin to help me move.

I vividly recall while preaching on one Sunday morning my youngest brother called concerning my sick parents. I immediately led the church in prayer. Handing the phone to my eldest son, I instructed him to call his uncle, my brother, for details. After the service, I was informed my mom was losing consciousness and my siblings were divided on the decision for her to seek professional medical care. My oldest sister, a nurse, checked on her, but mom's condition worsened after she left. My other sister, also a nurse, began to give instructions to our youngest siblings who were at the home of my parents caring for them. However, mom was too fragile. I sent a message to my siblings, asserting that despite their views, I was on the way to Jasper to take my mom to a hospital for medical care. This decision upset some of them.

My journey to Jasper, still in my church attire, was filled with urgency and prayer. While on my way, my youngest sister called to say mom had lost consciousness again. I insisted she call 911 and get her to a doctor, regardless of what anyone said. Turning on my emergency flashers, I sped down the highway, praying fervently. I couldn't help but plead with God, about the promises He made about my parents years ago. Despite my faith, I was deeply concerned about their spiritual well-being, as they hadn't cultivated a strong relationship with God, despite their upbringing in the church. I wanted to ensure I would be there to pray with my mom. As I drove, tears streamed down my face. I prayed so hard I began to lose my voice. I begged God to spare my mom's life until I arrived.

While speeding through Zavalla, Texas, I passed a police officer who was parked in their usual spot known for ticketing, to my surprise, I was not stopped. Given Zavalla's reputation for issuing multiple speeding tickets, I saw this as divine intervention.

My arrival at Christus Jasper Memorial Hospital was a moment I'll never forget. Upon arriving there, my youngest sister was already present. I was allowed by the staff to enter the room to see my mom. Seeing her so frail, her body weakened from not eating for days was saddening. We prayed together, with her faintly repeating the prayers and seeking God's forgiveness. Later, she expressed a desire to "go home," a phrase often spoken by those nearing death. Her eyes were glossy and dazed, and she appeared to show signs of dementia. I sat beside her, trying to provide comfort. She then asked about her grandchild, who we called, "JoJo." He's my nephew and often brought happiness and laughter to my parents whenever he came around. I knew this meant something, my mom wanted to feel joy and peace at that moment.

I continued to sit with her, praying, as she repeated her desire to go home. She mentioned unpaid bills and needing to go to the store, referring to tasks with my dad. I reassured her, saying, "It's okay mama, Kreshia has your debit card and information she will take care of it for you."

Hours later, the decision to airlift her to a hospital in Beaumont was made as her condition worsened. As I watched the medical team prepare her for the journey, I felt a mix of hope and sadness. By then, she had lost recognition of me and her surroundings. As the medical team placed her body on the gurney, I told her she was going to Beaumont and my eldest brother, would meet her there. Her confused and unresponsive look as they loaded her on that gurney will forever be etched in my memory.

I then left the hospital and waited inside my car until the medical team loaded her body into the helicopter. I sat there watching as the helicopter lifted her in the air, transporting her to the next hospital.

The subsequent days brought more challenges. The next day, my dad was admitted to the same hospital in Beaumont.

During mom's hospital stay, she remained sedated and unaware of the visits by my siblings and I. Dad, though conscious and alert, had slurred speech, making it difficult to comprehend him.

Then came the devastating news. On October 13, 2021, we received the news of mom's passing. I was in Lufkin at the time and drove two hours to Beaumont to see her one last time. At the hospital, her face looked tired. As I stood there staring at her, the finality of her departure began to sink in. I desired to pull back the blankets for a final look at her body, but I couldn't muster the strength. Alone in the room with her, I received a call from my youngest sister, Lakreshia, asking for pictures of her.

Watching the coroner arrive was a surreal moment. I was struck with reality. I watched them take her away, repeating to myself in disbelief, 'Mama is gone, mama is gone.' The echoing of these words in my mind felt like a hammer to my heart.

While emotional, I questioned God's purpose in revealing to me the dream about her death. My heart ached with the knowledge that both my parents were hospitalized, and now my mom was no longer with us.

Dad's health initially seemed to improve, but we kept the news of mom's death from him, hoping to shield him from further distress. We notified the staff not to inform him about mom's death.

However, the situation took another turn. Days later, I spoke with one of the caseworkers over the phone, and she stated that dad's health had taken a turn for the worse, and they believed it was because he knew that mom was dead. This information, and the way it was delivered, left me both disgusted and upset.

The day before mom's funeral, on October 22, 2021, we received death news for the second time. Dad had passed away just nine days after mom.

I vividly remember visiting him at the hospital the day before his death. His body was swollen, on a respirator, and covered in a large plastic-like bubble. It was a sight I had never seen before.

On the day of mom's funeral, we grieved not only for her but for our dad as well.

Returning to the funeral home the next week for our dad was an overwhelming experience, one that felt almost unreal. Losing both parents so close together was overwhelming, despite the prophetic warning. It was no longer a dream of prophetic intel, but now a reality.

After the death of my parents, I thought about my first grandchild, born that same year on July 4th, who had only met my parents once, adding another layer of sadness to the loss.

Reflecting on these events, I turned to scripture for comfort. When my parents passed just nine days apart - the number symbolic of new beginnings - it felt like a divine reflection of the recurring relationship between death and rebirth.

God began to lead me to 2 Samuel 7:12-13. Like Solomon who was the successor of his father, David, I felt God's call to continue the legacy my parents had left incomplete. Among my siblings, I was the only one with a grandchild who was born three months before their passing, symbolizing not just continuity in the face of loss, but the readiness of a new generation to embrace the charge ahead.

I believe one of the reasons God charged me with the call was because of certain qualities I had nurtured over time. He then began to remind me of those qualities. Honor, a virtue I upheld with my parents despite our differing spiritual connections; faithfulness, demonstrated through my steadfast dedication to my calling; and courage to defy norms, embodied in my role as the first female preacher in a family of traditionalists. These attributes, along with the symbolic birth of my grandchild, marked the beginning of a new era, ready for the responsibilities that lay ahead.

My role as the first female preacher in our family had always been met with resistance, yet it was a path God had ordained for me. Since I was the first female preacher in the family according to my father, I was an outlier, defying long-standing traditions and facing resistance. Yet, this was a journey God had prepared me for, equipping me to spiritually lead my family away from false beliefs.

Although over time I have received prophetic words concerning my role in helping my family, this realization wasn't immediate but emerged as a profound responsibility over time.

Feeling called to be the successor, I recognized the divine appointment in being chosen among my seven siblings to uphold our lineage. Increasingly more, I felt the call to be that successor, to complete what my parents had left unfinished. This selection was not about superiority but about a divine appointment, a recognition of the qualities I demonstrated and the role I was destined to fulfill.

Though my parents believed in attending worship services occasionally, they did not cultivate a close relationship with God. Nonetheless, I honored them per biblical teachings, a gesture of respect and love that transcended our spiritual differences.

It took over a year after their passing for me to fully comprehend the message behind their deaths. My charge also extended beyond my family to challenging the way people thought about religion, as referenced in Jeremiah 1:10 to break down barriers.

As the first woman preacher in my lineage, I was already defying norms, my mission expanded to reshaping the entire framework of faith.

God's decision to choose me, the third child, defied traditional expectations of birthright succession, emphasizing the divine nature of my calling. This was a clear indication of my role in breaking generational curses and setting new spiritual precedents.

Despite occasional stumbles, I remained committed to my path. I understood the passing of one generation is necessary for the new to emerge. In this way, death acts as a catalyst for rebirth and progression. As a link between the past, present, and future, I am called to sow seeds of faith, dismantle generational curses, and establish a new legacy of spiritual integrity.

In all of this, I've learned to trust in the strategic ways of God, accepting that His plans are not always for us to understand immediately but to trust and obey. This belief has guided me through my spiritual awakening and continues to be the foundation of my journey.

As I adjusted to these new realities of my parent's death, I was faced with yet another loss during that time. An elderly Deacon from my former church, whom I communicated with regularly, passed away in October. He often checked on me and my family. His funeral was during the time I was preparing the arrangements for my mom. I was consumed by my mother's burial arrangements, so I was unable to attend his funeral. Or properly grieve the loss of him. I believed he sincerely loved me and my family.

I held on to the memories of him while he was alive. He had traveled to Lufkin on Tuesdays for doctor appointments. He would let me know when he was coming to town, but due to my schedule, we were never able to meet for lunch. One day in August, I decided to make time for that long-overdue lunch. I figured since I was in the process of moving and no longer working this would be the perfect time to meet. However, when I called, his phone went straight to voicemail, which was odd. Later I saw on Facebook that he was hospitalized, so I reached out to check on his condition.

About a week later, I received his hospital room information and managed to speak briefly with him by phone. That conversation would be our last before his passing in October.

His death added to my already grieving spirit, creating a silent pain, a profound sorrow not visible to others, but deeply felt by me.

Experiencing three deaths in one month felt like a fire burning within my heart that I could not extinguish. The intensity of this pain was not something I could simply extinguish, but rather something I had to learn to carry and manage. I had to develop coping mechanisms in an attempt to alleviate the grief. To soothe the ache, I turned to journaling, letting pen and paper hold the sorrows I couldn't voice. Writing became my quiet therapy, a release in written words.

During this time, I experienced the loss of my parents, I lost my relationship with my siblings, I lost my house, I lost my business, and I left my two sons behind with their father. The multitude of these losses was a lot to bear in 2021. I grappled with a deep sense of emptiness and confusion, struggling to comprehend why I was facing so much turmoil at once. I pleaded with God for strength and understanding.

I found myself questioning the prophetic words I had once passionately believed in. The support I had expected from loved ones was noticeably absent, leaving me to wonder about their silence. Internally, I felt a growing weakness, contrary to the strong persona I was known for. Despite my contributions to various churches, where I had served and blessed many, their response now seemed distant and unresponsive. This lack of empathy from my spiritual community was hurtful, leaving me feeling isolated in my time of need.

In my moments of despair, I questioned the timing of these trials. "Oh God, my faith is shifting," I cried out, fearing the loss of the one thing that had always given me strength--my faith. I was overwhelmed with emotions, wondering why those I had supported in their times of need were now seemingly oblivious to my pain. Flashes of hurt and confusion filled my thoughts. Prayer, which had always been my solace, became a struggle, as my mind was clouded with distractions.

In my search for solace and a prayer partner, I reached out to a prophetess in Kirbyville, Texas. Her prayers and guidance offered me a momentary respite.

During our call, she talked about giving me five hundred dollars to buy food and pay for two days in a hotel. Surprisingly, she sent me seven hundred dollars instead. I didn't ask for financial help nor did I insinuate it during the call, but she felt moved by the spirit to do this. With her help, I was able to stay three days in a hotel.

It was a reminder from God that, even in unfavorable situations, He still favors me, as it's rare for someone to give so generously without being asked. This act of kindness was a ray of hope in a period of deep sorrow, reaffirming my faith in God's provision.

After the death of my parents, my siblings and I became divided, just as God revealed to me in a dream in June 2021 about a funeral, which I now realize was my mother's. I found myself faced with accusations from some of my siblings about my role in handling our mother's funeral arrangements. Despite my efforts to honor her desires, I was accused of lying about being entrusted with her burial arrangements. They seemed to have forgotten my previous text messages in which I detailed our parents' desires. I took proactive steps to manage our parents' affairs, including contacting the Social Security Administration to ensure payments sent to my parent's bank account would cease. However, no matter what I did, nothing seemed to mend the tension.

The family discord escalated when I was wrongfully accused of removing a safe from our parents' house. The safe was too heavy for me to carry alone, and ironically, I had misplaced its combination during my move. This misplaced code was even surprising for me because I'm known for being well-organized. Besides my parents, I was the only person who knew the combination. My siblings' assumptions were not only hurtful but also illogical, given my inability to move the safe and the lost combination. Some of my siblings continued with false accusations, even about money, without any proof. This unfounded suspicion led to a further division in our family, with three of us against five.

Despite my attempts to share God's guidance with them, they mocked and doubted me. Some of my siblings even remarked, "You are not the only person whom God speaks to," dismissing any message I received from God. I chose to turn to God for comfort, refusing to engage in baseless accusations. I desired peace, and I refused to be falsely accused in my innocence. Because they refused to engage in healthy conversations, I chose to disengage.

I was hurt by the division in our family, especially as I tried to respect my mother's desires while dealing with my siblings' disbelief and personal feelings toward me. The false claim about the safety box both hurt and upset me. They didn't remember that I couldn't move it or that I had lost the combination. The mistrust hurt and angered me.

At first, I wondered why they would think such things about me. I didn't have a reputation in the family to be dishonest. I began to understand that their perceptions were not about me but about the enemy's purpose to keep us separated and prevent unity.

Despite these challenges, I remained committed to the ministry God had given me. Despite my emotional rollercoaster, I recognized what was happening for me was far greater than what was happening to me. Everything had a purpose, and every behavior had meaning.

The spirit within me was determined to move forward.

Dedicated to my calling, I continued driving from Louisiana to Lufkin twice every month on Sundays to lead worship services, despite the modest offerings which often were less than twenty dollars. However, serving God was my primary focus, not financial gain. Our first in-person worship service took place recently that year in July. Only months before the death of my parents and my move to Louisiana.

Before we began our first in-person services I received my license to pastor and was affirmed as a prophetess in June 2021 in Baton Rouge, Louisiana. Although, my active involvement in ministry dates back to 2009. This affirmation was not the beginning of a new journey, but a recognition of the path I had been on for years.

With the new license, it would enhance my ability to serve and lead more within the community.

Following each service, I encountered individuals seeking prayers and support, particularly those in need of food. Despite my limited resources, I provided groceries, assisted by my two sons who helped distribute them. This act of giving was a testament to my faith, even as my savings dwindled. I did this while I wasn't generating any income, and my bank account was diminishing.

Despite the dwindling state of my bank account, I didn't let my circumstances define my appearance. The spirit of God endowed me with a supernatural strength that radiated through my being, beautifying my appearance. So, I did not look like what I was going through. God remained my stronghold, providing for me in the most unexpected ways. I could no longer afford the beauty treatments I once did, like getting my hair, nails, and feet done. I adapted by painting white tips on my naturally long nails appearing to have a professional look. Additionally, others prompted by God, would reach out to offer me hair or nail treatments making it so the changes in my life weren't reflected in my appearance. It was as if I were still maintaining my usual beauty routines. It looked as if I was still being well-maintained.

This experience taught me a profound lesson: as long as I stayed committed to God's work, He would fulfill the desires of my heart, as promised in Psalm 37:4, "Delight yourself in the Lord and He will give you the desires of your heart."

My journey was marked by unexpected twists, financial hardship, and emotional turmoil. Still, I remained unwavering in my faith and determination to carry out God's plan, even when it led me through challenging times. My story is one of resilience, determination, and unwavering faith in God's guidance and provision.

In 2021, I faced the most challenging year of my life. It brought losses that felt overwhelming, from the sudden passing of my parents to the fractures in my family relationships. The weight of it all was heavy, leaving me searching for answers. There were moments when I felt like I was drowning in despair, but little did I understand that God was leading me through the fire to respond with His refining fire.

With every loss, I began to develop strategies to find victory. Each setback and each challenge taught me the value of persistence and unwavering determination. Even when the odds seemed overwhelming with every bit of little strength in me, I clung to my faith as the steadfast anchor in my life.

It was through these trials that I recognized that even in the depths of despair, God's guidance and provision were still present. In times of tribulation, I was reminded of 1 Peter 1:7, which reveals that our faith, more precious than gold, is refined through trials, ultimately leading to praise, glory, and a stronger spirit. Just as gold is purified in the intense heat of a furnace, our faith is strengthened and purified through the fires of life's adversities. These trials test the genuineness of our faith and reveal its enduring quality. The pressure identified my true value. The end result is not only a stronger and more resilient faith but also a deeper connection with God, as I learned to rely on Him more for guidance, strength, and provision during those trying times.

These revelations brought a newfound clarity and purpose to my life, reinforcing my commitment to my spiritual journey and my trust in God's plan.

Chapter 8

Emerging From Flames

And I will bring the third part through the fire, and will refine them as silver is refined, and will try them as gold is tried: they shall call on my name, and I will hear them: I will say, It is my people: and they shall say, The Lord is my God. -Zechariah 13:9

As the tumultuous year of 2021 drew to a close, my time in Louisiana became a defining period of personal growth. The trials I faced there, from living away from what I had always known, to dealing with family issues and unjust allegations, were not mere obstacles but stepping stones. They shaped a deeper understanding of my independence, which had always been a cornerstone of my character. This chapter, while challenging, was instrumental in revealing the true extent of my resilience and faith.

Believing that every journey has its purpose, I recognized that this phase in Louisiana was crucial. It wasn't a detour but a necessary path on my life's map, leading me to where I needed to be. As I embraced 2022, it wasn't just about leaving behind the struggles of the past year. It was about carrying forward the lessons learned, and the strength gained, to reach our ultimate destinations.

After walking through the inferno of 2021, I eagerly anticipated new beginnings for 2022. Embracing the idea that some paths in life are one-way, with no detours, I was ready to embark on this new phase of my journey. I remained hopeful and optimistic about the future.

One early morning in April 2022 around 5 AM, while on a prayer conference call, a supernatural experience occurred just as the service was concluding. A cloudy presence filled the entire living room where I lay. A peaceful presence began to fall on me. In that moment God spoke to me. He assured me that the intense spiritual warfare I had endured for years was giving way to a new season, one where I wouldn't endure the same battles as before. God was promising a change, this time, the struggles of the past wouldn't repeat. Although challenges would come, they would not mirror those I had previously encountered.

This manifestation, cloud appearance, was too immense and awe-inspiring. In that moment God offered reassurance and a promise.

Two months later in June 2022, I had made significant progress. I secured my apartment and began working from home as a Senior Medicare Agent for Company AS. My new home was beautiful, complete with a pond, waterfall, and a variety of amenities like a fitness center, business center, and pool. This serene environment was in perfect harmony with the vision God had shown me back in 2021, a vision that was now unfolding into reality.

The property manager played a pivotal role in this transition, helping me find an apartment that was a perfect fit for my needs. He was instrumental in finding me an ideal apartment downstairs with a fireplace. To my surprise, the apartment was not only fully renovated but also less expensive than what I was first told.

Everything inside was brand new - from the fresh coat of paint on the walls to the modern light fixtures, new flooring, all new appliances, new ceiling fans, countertops, toilets, and cabinetry. To add to the blessing, the manager generously offered free electricity for the first month.

My new home was a manifestation of the dream – living in a gated community, just as I had dreamed of in 2021.

From my storage in Lufkin, I brought only a bedroom set, three TVs, and some decor. The apartment came well-equipped with stainless steel appliances including a stove, microwave, refrigerator, and dishwasher. The apartment also came furnished with a new washer and dryer.

Despite not having much furniture or a dining room set, I wasn't bothered by the minimalism of my living situation. It was peaceful, especially since I was there alone, awaiting my oldest son's arrival in July.

The transition was swift; I moved in mid-June on a Friday and by Monday, I began working.

Financially, I was still recovering from the transition and the losses I endured. For extra income, I also did commercial inspections in Louisiana. I had begun to meticulously plan to address the bills I had fallen behind on. I continued with other side hustles alongside my job at Company AS.

Two months into the role as a senior medicare agent, another company called Company AC, which I had never contacted nor had filled out an application, reached out to me. They had found my details in a database and offered me a remote contract position as a Licensed Benefits Counselor with better pay. Although it didn't include commission, it seemed like a better opportunity because the pay was an additional ten dollars more per hour than Company AS. This new position as a Licensed Benefit Counselor was set to start in September 2022.

I was about to start working at Company AC, so I gave Company AS a ten-day notice to resign. However, instead of waiting ten days, my supervisor ended my position immediately because the position involved sales. I planned to use my remaining paid time off during my last days at work, however, the company's policy was that accrued time had to be used before leaving. Therefore, it could not be paid on my last payroll check. However, in a surprising turn of events, Company AS later compensated me for this unused time - an act that defied their policy and I knew this was a clear sign of God's favor in my life.

Around the same time, I just re-enrolled at Stephen F. Austin State University to complete my bachelor's degree, which I had begun in 2014 and ended in 2016. Returning to college after a six-year break was both exciting and a chance for a new beginning. I returned as a senior, with only two semesters left. This return to college wasn't just about earning a degree; it was about fulfilling a commitment to myself, a promise to complete what I had started.

In August 2022, one day while working at my desk, my journey took a spiritual turn. Immediately I felt a compelling need to pray against a suicidal spirit, it was a moment of divine intervention. I immediately knelt on the floor to begin praying. After praying, I sent a message to a family member, to let her know all of a sudden I felt a strong need to pray for someone who wants to commit suicide. Her response was unexpected; she identified herself as the one struggling with the suicidal spirit, and I was led to pray for her. This revelation was an obvious reminder that the power of prayer often extends beyond our understanding, reaching those who need it most, sometimes even ourselves.

I would soon realize that this prayer was not only just for her.

That same month, my son returned from the store with a troubling question: "Mom, where's your car?" His observant eyes had noticed the absence of my BMW X3 which was not parked in its usual spot. I knew immediately that it had been repossessed. This wasn't entirely unexpected; I had dreamed of this happening. The repossession hit me like a physical and emotional tsunami. It felt as if a massive weight had been suddenly thrust upon my shoulders, and a heavy spirit surrounded me. The loss felt like a blow, similar to a physical punch that knocked the breath out of me. In that moment, engulfed in emotion, I pondered over the relentless nature of my challenges. Despite my efforts to catch up on my bills, I was three months behind, and my recent conversation with the customer service representative, where I had attempted to negotiate a partial payment, had been denied.

Overcome with emotion and the weight of my circumstances, I collapsed to my knees, contemplating suicide. This thought hadn't crossed my mind since I was a teenager. Without realization, I found myself in the same location on the floor where I had previously prayed against the suicidal spirit now pleading for mercy and contemplating drastic measures. While kneeling there, crying and pleading with God, I reminded myself of the promises I held onto, even as I faced this crushing loss. The intensity of my emotions drove me to a closet, where I began to search through important documents, including my insurance policies. I then explained their significance to my oldest son, ensuring he understood their location and importance. In a moment of deep vulnerability, I sent messages to my other two children, detailing my banking information and the location of our insurance policies. My children had no idea about my reasoning for doing this.

I went to my bathroom and opened the medicine cabinet, searching for acetaminophen. I then grabbed a pill bottle to begin to contemplate swallowing all the pills. I wanted it to be instant. I began to debate within myself. "What if the pills don't work?" I thought, "And I'm found still alive." It was a battle within me, torn between prayer and a spirit of despair. There I was, a person who had spent years praying for others, now struggling with the idea of taking my own life.

The struggle within me was inescapable. I considered using my gun. I grabbed my gun and then dropped to the floor on my knees but was deterred by the fear of pain and the uncertain outcome. My mind raced with thoughts of my children, the prophetic words I had received, the promises God had made to me, and my unfulfilled aspirations.

Despite my usual strength, I felt an overwhelming sense of weakness and anger at my vulnerability. Scriptures began to flood my mind, and I realized that the suicidal spirit I had previously been praying against was manifesting within me.

I had locked myself in the room, uncertain of my next steps and not wanting my son to witness it.

Through prayer and introspection, I recognized that the spirit of despair within me had been dormant, waiting for an opportunity to surface. This realization was symbolic of understanding a chronic illness; it doesn't manifest overnight but builds up over time, triggered by certain events.

The emergence of this dormant spirit was a call to action. It was time to confront and dismantle it, so it could no longer hold power over me. I realized this spirit had been with me since my teenage years, lying dormant, waiting for the right moment to emerge. The revelation was clear: when old spirits arise, it doesn't mean they have recently appeared. They were dormant, waiting for an opportunity. I had to understand that God had given me the authority and power to pray against this spirit and to renounce it. This was to ensure it would never return and then replace it with the blood of Christ.

To renounce this spirit meant I needed to break the covenant, the illegal right it claimed over me. Once this covenant is broken and replaced with the blood of Christ, the spirit loses its dormant status and its grip on my life. It's one thing to pray, but another to pray and actively renounce.

I won the battle against the urge to end my life, a victory that came from deep within, fortified by my faith and the realization that my life was worth more than any temporary setback. This victory was more than just overcoming a moment of weakness; it was a triumph over a dormant spirit that had lurked within me for years.

Shortly after this spiritual warfare, I had a conversation with the prophetess from Kirbyville, who revealed that God spoke to her that I would reclaim my BMW.

Miraculously, just over six months later, I was able to purchase another BMW X3. The process was smooth, and the fact that the company only required my driver's license and social security card, without needing proof of my employment, was nothing short of divine intervention. It was evident of God's favor and presence in my life that the repossession of my previous car didn't appear on my credit report. This vehicle, purchased from the same company but in a different city, and shipped like the previous one, symbolized a well-deserved divine blessing.

This chapter of my life was a testament to the supernatural power of God, a reminder that even in what may seem to be our toughest hours, He is working in ways we cannot comprehend.

Each challenge I faced was like a fire, fierce yet cleansing. These trials, like flames, burned away what was old, leaving me stronger. I emerged not weakened but purified, reshaped by the very hardships I went through. This experience taught me something profound: the hidden suicidal spirit inside me was like a hidden spark, ready to ignite when the time was right. It reminded me of how diabetes doesn't happen suddenly but builds up over time. Just like these spiritual challenges that lay dormant, waiting for a trigger.

These experiences taught me about true resilience – it's not just surviving the fire but coming out of it transformed and fortified.

Conclusion

The Bible recounts in Daniel 3 that when Shadrach, Meshach, and Abednego were cast into the fiery furnace, nothing bad happened to them. Their bodies remained unharmed—no hair was singed, and their garments bore no trace of smoke. People often remark to me that I don't appear to have endured the challenges I've faced. I explain that it's not about my outward appearance; it's because God's constant presence shielded me from harm in life's trials. Just like the Bible describes a 'fourth man walking' with Shadrach, Meshach, and Abednego in their fiery trial, I too sensed a comforting and guiding presence during my challenging moments. I understand that as long as this 'fourth man' is with me in my trials, I can walk through anything!

Entering a new season in life, as Scripture in Isaiah 43:18-19 says, 'Forget the former things; do not dwell on the past. See, I am doing a new thing! Now it springs up; do you not perceive it?' This change is similar to the natural cycle of leaves withering in winter to make way for the blooming of beautiful, colorful flowers in spring. It's a time when all things are made new, symbolizing renewal and transformation. It's important to understand that losses are often precursors to victories. They teach and prepare us for success, much like a basketball team after losing to an opponent who then studies their plays to learn their behaviors and strategies. This preparation is aimed at securing a win in future encounters.

While scripture teaches that in God there are no true losses, my journey has personally shown me what appears as loss is often a disguised blessing, preparing me for greater victories. Letting go of what we are familiar and comfortable with can be challenging. It's hard to be uprooted from one place and moved to another. However, as God moves us from one elevation to another, He prunes us meticulously, knowing exactly what and where to cut.

We often make the mistake of thinking we know what is best for ourselves, similar to an untrained person attempting surgery with a scalpel. In contrast, a skilled surgeon, educated and experienced, knows precisely where to make incisions. Similarly, God knows what to prune in our lives to foster our betterment.

In moments of emotion and limited understanding, it's crucial to remember that God is in complete control, even when it feels like we are not. Every experience molds us into who we are today. The experience of divorce, while challenging, became a profound lesson in the art of letting go, teaching me the value of resilience and the strength found in new beginnings. These things I clung to were holding me back, so God stepped in to prune them from my life.

The fires needed to be set to get me to move. Each time fire was set to aspects of my life, it caused me to move to a different position. Leaving the ministry wasn't a total loss; it left me with valuable lessons. Without opposition, I would have stayed there, stagnant, not progressing to where I am today. If I had never moved to Lufkin, I would never have received the outreach marketing position, which gave me invaluable experience in meeting community and government officials. This, combined with the fact that I had devoted so much time to being a wife and mother that I had prioritized those roles over my faith, which made it clear that God needed to separate me from that environment. He placed me in a foreign land, away from familiar surroundings, so I would not be easily accessed and could focus more on my faith. I didn't realize it at the time, but all of this was part of God's purposeful setup, as every fire had a purpose and every trial had meaning. If He had not acted like a bulldozer, removing things within and around me, I would have remained stagnant.

The scripture reminds us that God is a consuming fire, adept at knowing what type of fire to use for our refinement. He understands what we need and orchestrates our lives accordingly, despite our limited comprehension and attempts to align our thoughts with His.

Looking forward, I embrace this new beginning. As I have learned, God always blesses us through our journeys, much like Job, who received much more than he lost. I eagerly anticipate the new things in my life – a new husband, friendships, connections, businesses, and increases in all areas of my life. It's vital to realize that God never loses control, even when things seem chaotic.

This is not a time of sadness, complaint, or blame, but a time to celebrate the newness of life, like a flower blooming or a caterpillar transforming into a butterfly. Like Shadrach, Meshach, and Abednego, who in Daniel 3:27 emerged unscathed from the fire, I too have passed through my trials without harm. These experiences have not left me damaged. I do not bear the marks of my past struggles because God has seen me through them. The scripture assures us that God has plans to give us hope and a future, turning our endings into new beginnings.

Going through many of these trials throughout the years took a toll on my mental state. However, remaining prayerful in God and constantly going to Him for strategy is what kept me. I never had to take any medication because God is my physician. Without Him, I would not have made it.

In closing, I realize that the losses of yesterday are but catalysts to tomorrow's triumphs. As I move forward, I carry with me a renewed spirit, ready to embrace the abundant blessings that await. My journey continues, ever guided by faith and the promise of renewed beginnings. To be continued…

But He knows the way that I take; when He has tested me,
I will come forth as gold. - Job 23:10

The Untold
Stories of Survival

In the heart's storage, secrets tightly bound,
The untold stories of survival, unspoken, yet profound.
Like birds in cages yearning to be free,
These stories of strength and courage yearn to flee.

Amid the flames, in trials' fiery heat,
They weathered the smoke, stood tall, complete.
For what a fire doesn't consume, it purifies,
And within these stories, resilient spirits rise.

With wings unseen, they soared above the blaze,
Their resolve unbroken in the darkest days.
Each life a testament to survival's might,
Guided by a flickering, unwavering light.

So let us share, let us unveil,
The strength within us, the courage that prevails.
For in these stories we may find,
The beauty in the ashes, the strength in the mind.

"The Untold Stories of Survival," we now declare,
Are not just stories but a testament to dare.
To speak, to share, to release, to get better,
For in our stories, we find our wings, together.

- LaDonyae Thomas

About The Author

LaDonyae Thomas grew up in a small community in Texas among eight siblings. She is a true visionary and multifaceted individual who operates with a strong prophetic voice, provides wise counsel, and is known as a dynamic prayer warrior.

She balances her roles as an author, entrepreneur, mentor, life coach, grandmother, mother of three, and licensed pastor.

LaDonyae holds a Bachelor of Science degree in Human Science with a concentration in Human Development and Family Studies. She accepted the call to the ministry beginning in 2009 affirming her commitment to nurturing and guiding others.

Her literary aspirations originated in 1995 with a love for poetry. This passion for writing was later produced in 2017 with the publishing of her first book, *I'm A Christian But Broke: 7 Biblical Truths Why Christians Are Not Prosperous*. LaDonyae finds inspiration in her quotes like, "Continue to press play" and "God will never take you through without blessing you," which speak to her optimistic resilience.

She founded Faith Builders International Ministries to nurture spiritual growth and uplift communities where the mission is, "Building Faith, Uprooting Barriers," inspired by Jeremiah 1:10, further strengthening her impact as a faith leader. She is one of commitment, strength, resilience, and persistence.

Readers can explore more of LaDonyae's works on her website, thepenofareadywriter.com, and Facebook page, Author LaDonyae Thomas. Her multifaceted story stands as a testament to the power of enduring faith and the transformative nature of embracing life's tribulations.